Generative AI

The cybersecurity landscape is changing, for sure. For example, one of the oldest threat variants is that of phishing. It evolved in the early 1990s, but even today it is still being used as a primary threat variant and has now become much more sophisticated, covert, and stealthy in nature. For example, it can be used to launch ransomware, social engineering, and extortion attacks.

The advent of Generative AI is making this much worse. For example, a cyberattacker can now use something like ChatGPT to craft the content for phishing emails that are so convincing that it is almost impossible to tell the difference between what is real and what is fake. This is also clearly evident in the use of deepfakes, where fake images of real people are replicated to create videos to lure unsuspecting victims to a fake website.

But Generative AI can also be used for good, to combat phishing attacks. This is the topic of this book, and we cover the following:

- A review of phishing
- A review of AI, Neural Networks, and Machine Learning
- A review of Natural Language Processing, Generative AI, and the Digital Person
- A proposed solution as to how Generative AI can combat phishing attacks as they relate to Privileged Access accounts

Ravindra Das is a technical writer in the cybersecurity realm. He also does cybersecurity consulting on the side through his private practice, ML Tech, Inc. He holds the Certified in Cybersecurity certification from ISC2.

Cyber Shorts Series

Forthcoming books:

Ransomware
Penetration Testing and Contingency Planning
Ravindra Das

Deploying the Zero Trust Framework in MSFT Azure
Ravindra Das

Generative AI
Phishing and Cybersecurity Metrics
Ravindra Das

For more information about the series:

Generative AI
Phishing and Cybersecurity Metrics

Ravindra Das

CRC Press
Taylor & Francis Group
Boca Raton London New York

CRC Press is an imprint of the
Taylor & Francis Group, an **informa** business

Designed cover image: © Shutterstock

First edition published 2025
by CRC Press
2385 NW Executive Center Drive, Suite 320, Boca Raton FL 33431

and by CRC Press
4 Park Square, Milton Park, Abingdon, Oxon, OX14 4RN

CRC Press is an imprint of Taylor & Francis Group, LLC

© 2025 Ravindra Das

ISBN: 9781032820965 (hbk)
ISBN: 9781032822686 (pbk)
ISBN: 9781003503781 (ebk)

DOI: 10.1201/9781003503781

Typeset in Caslon
by Newgen Publishing UK

This book is dedicated to my Lord and Savior, Jesus Christ, the Grand Designer of the Universe, and to my parents, Dr. Gopal Das and Mrs. Kunda Das.

My loving cats, Fifi and Bubu.

This book is also dedicated to:

Richard and Gwynda Bowman

Jaya Chandra

Tim Auckley

Patricia Bornhofen

Ashish Das

Contents

Acknowledgments

I would like to thank Barbara Dawson and Ms. Gabriella Williams, my editor, for making this book a reality.

1

INTRODUCTION TO PHISHING

As we move deeper into 2024, there are many events that are totally unprecedented. These are political, financial, and global situations that are transpiring. But to make things even scarier, some of the worst things that are happening at the present time are the cyberthreats that are coming out. For example, gone are the days when threat variants were primitive and more or less predictable.

Probably the best example of this is phishing. As most of us know, this is probably the oldest threat vector around. It first emerged in the 1990s, but it did not become an official threat until America Online (AOL) was attacked. This was the most widely used platform for web surfing and for communicating via email and instant messaging (IM). Back at that time, high speed Internet was just starting to come out, and it was the traditional dial-up modem that was being used to connect AOL to an Internet service provider.

In fact, here is a chronological timeline of just how phishing evolved back then:

- The concept of phishing can be traced back to the early 1990s via America Online (AOL). A group of hackers and pirates who came together and called themselves the warez community are considered the first true "phishers".
- In an early scam, they created an algorithm that allowed them to generate random credit card numbers. When a real card was matched, they were able to create an account and spam others in the AOL community.
- By 1995, AOL was able to stop the random credit card generators, but the warez group moved on to other methods, pretending to be AOL employees and messaging people

DOI: 10.1201/9781003503781-1

via AOL Instant Messenger for their information in social engineering attacks.

- On January 2, 1996, the word "phishing" was first posted in a Usenet group dedicated to America Online.
- By the mid-1990s phishers switched to email communications, which were easy to create, cheap to send out, and made it nearly impossible for them to get caught. In September 2003, phishers began registering domains that were similar to popular companies such as Yahoo (yahoo-billing.com) and eBay (ebay-fulfillment.com).
- In October 2003, PayPal users were impacted by the Mimail virus. When they clicked on a link contained in a phishing email, a popup window appeared claiming to be coming from PayPal. It instructed them to enter their username/password, which was immediately sent to the cyberattackers.
- In 2004, voters for presidential candidate John Kerry received an official-looking email, asking them to donate via an authentic-looking (but malicious) link. It turned out to be a scam operating in both India and Texas that had no connection to the Kerry campaign.

Phishing has always been done by email, and up until now, the signs of it were obvious. Here are some examples:

- There is an unfamiliar tone or greeting to the email message.
- There are many grammar and spelling errors.
- There are numerous inconsistencies in the email address (primarily the sender), links, and domain names in the email message itself.
- There is a strong threat or a sense of urgency to the email message.
- There are suspicious attachments included (primarily those of .XLS and .DOC file extensions).
- They make unusual requests that are out of the norm.
- The email message is short and sweet in order to play tricks on your memory.
- The recipient did not initiate the conversation; very often this is a hook to inform the recipient he or she has won a prize, will

qualify for a prize if they reply to the email, or will benefit from a discount by clicking on a link or opening an attachment.
- There is often a request for credentials (such as your username/ password), payment information (like your credit card number), or other personal details.

So, in other words, given these indicators, people could more or less tell if they had received a phishing based email, and assuming that they were proactive about it could avoid being harmed by it. But as time went on, and as technology further developed, so did the mindset of the cyberattacker. For instance, many new variants of phishing came out, and here are some examples to illustrate this fact:

- The average cost to a business in one year is a staggering $3.86 million.
- Business email compromise (aka BEC, a variant of phishing) has cost companies around the world $12.5 billion.
- The largest phishing attack was on a healthcare organization.
- Spear phishing emails (yet another variant) cost $16 million.
- Phishing attacks heavily target the financial sector – it costs one financial firm $18 million in a single year just to recover from phishing attacks.
- It costs $135/hour for a business to recover from a phishing attack; if you are sued because your company was hit by a phishing attack, it will cost you $260/hour just in legal fees.
- Identity theft protection services can cost as much as $9.99 per employee per month.
- If you have a call center, and they have to field calls answering questions about a phishing attack, it will cost your company $14.53/hour.
- Phishing victims have to be notified at least once by snail mail that they have potentially become a phishing victim. This costs, on average, $1 per letter. That may not sound like a lot, but costs add up if you have to send out thousands or even a million of these letters.
- Phishing attacks have risen by 65% from 2015 to 2016.

Although these may seem like the worst threat variants possible, the COVID-19 pandemic actually made things far worse. Cyberattackers became much more cunning and deceptive in how they sent out their phishing emails. For example, during this time period, many people around the world were experiencing the highest anxiety levels possible – and rightfully so. The cyberattacker literally preyed upon this human emotion by crafting stealthy messages offering free information on how to stay safe from COVID-19.

Very often, the unsuspecting victim was conned into clicking on a phony link (which is one of the biggest telltale signs of a phishing based email, along with downloading malicious attachments – most notably those of Microsoft Word, Microsoft PowerPoint, Microsoft Excel [in these particular cases, macros were the culprit of the malicious payloads], Adobe Acrobat Reader PDF files, etc.). Once the victim was on this phony website, they would then be lured into submitting their username/password combination to get the free information.

Another version of this was also known as "domain squatting". According to Wikipedia, it can be technically defined as follows:

> Domain squatting, also known as cybersquatting, is the practice of registering, trafficking in, or using an Internet domain name with the bad faith intent to profit from the goodwill of a trademark belonging to someone else.

In the context of domain names, cybersquatters typically register domain names that are identical or similar to trademarks of well-known companies or brands. They then hope to sell the domain names to the trademark owners for a profit or to use the domain names to redirect traffic to their websites, which may be malicious or spammy.

Cybersquatting can involve various deceptive practices, such as:

- Registering domain names that are confusingly similar to the trademarks of well-known companies or brands.
- Using domain names to redirect traffic to malicious websites.
- Selling domain names to trademark owners at a premium.

Let us illustrate this with an example. As we all know, Walmart is one of the largest retail stores here in the United States (and possibly even the world). Their legitimate URL address is as follows:

www.walmart.com/

In a Domain Squatting attack, the cyberattacker will actually register a domain that is very similar looking. An example of this is as follows:

www.wal-mart.com/
or
www.wallmart.com/

The idea behind getting one of these extremely similar looking names is to create a phony and malicious website. The idea is that the unsuspecting victim will not pay attention to this hard-to-notice, altered domain name, and simply go to it. This is also the very same thing that happened during the COVID-19 pandemic. Cyberattackers from all over the world were registering these kinds of domains of legitimate charities (such as the International Committee of the Red Cross) and health organizations (such as the World Health Organization) and creating fictitious websites.

Once a phishing based email was then sent to the unsuspecting victim, he or she would then be conned into clicking on the Domain Squatting link, log into an account, and make a donation. But of course, this was totally illegitimate, as the money that was transferred over would then be sent to a phony, offshore account, most likely in the location of a nation state actor, most notably Russia, China, North Korea, etc.

Then once the money was received, it was very difficult to try to get the money back. But these days, federal law enforcement agencies such as the United States Secret Service and the Federal Bureau of Investigation (FBI) are doing a much better job in tracking the sent funds and retrieving them for the victim. Also, financial institutions here in the United States are doing a far better job in identifying and stopping illegitimate wire transfers as well.

But after the COVID-19 pandemic peaked and retreated, phishing became far worse. It became so in three ways:

- Ransomware.
- The Dark Web.
- Extortion attacks.

Let us examine each of these separately, as they are deemed right now to be the worst forms of phishing variants:

Ransomware

Most of us have heard about ransomware. But the technical definition of it is as follows:

> Ransomware is a type of malware that holds a victim's data or device hostage, threatening to keep it locked – or worse – unless the victim pays a ransom to the attacker.[1]

Ransomware also stems from phishing. This is so because the malicious payload usually comes from the downloading of an attachment (as just reviewed), or from a phony link. But it could also be the case that the victim has not downloaded all of the requisite software patches and upgrades to their device, and thus a backdoor can be created through which a cyberattacker can enter covertly and, from there, deliver the ransomware payload. But however it is deployed, the results can be disastrous, if not catastrophic. In its simplest form, the malicious payload will merely lock the device of the victim, and encrypt all of the files that reside within it. In order to unlock the device and decrypt the files, the cyberattacker will often ask for a ransom payment to be made, typically in the form of a virtual currency such as Bitcoin.

The primary reason why the cyberattacker wants the payment to be made in this way is so that they cannot be tracked nearly as easily. If actual cash were to be used in this regard, it can be marked, and this will give law enforcement (such as the Secret Service and/or the FBI) a much greater chance of tracking down the perpetrator.

While it is tempting for the victim to make the ransom payment, there are many downsides to this. First and foremost, if payment is made by the victim, the chances are much greater that the cyberattacker could strike them again, and this time around, ask for even more money. Second, if a ransom payment is actually made, there is no guarantee that the decryption algorithms will be sent to the victim by the cyberattacker. Third, depending upon where the cyberattacker is actually located (such as Russia, China, North Korea, etc.) it could even be considered an act of treason against the United States if such payment is made.

This fact was established by the United States Treasury Department's Office of Foreign Assets Control (also known as the OFAC). More detail about this can be found at:

https://ofac.treasury.gov/

More information about ransomware payments and the impacts of United States federal law can be found at:

http://cyberresources.solutions/GenAI_Book/Law_Ransomw
are.pdf

In a worst-case scenario, if the ransom payment is really high, the victim can procure the services of a broker in order to negotiate with the cyberattacker to bring the ransom payment down. But this too can cost money and is not always very successful.

Figure 1.1 depicts the anatomy of a ransomware attack:
So now the question arises: How do you protect yourself from becoming a victim of a ransomware attack? Well, there are two ways to go about this:

1) Create Backups On Premises:

- This is one of the most basic rules in cybersecurity. Backups should be created all the time. That way, you can restore the mission critical datasets in a very quick fashion, so that your business does not suffer a lot of downtime. There are three distinct ways to do this: You can create a tape backup, you can do it in the Cloud, or you can use a combination of both. But whatever you decide to do, you should always maintain backups on site and off site. In this regard, there are three kinds of backups which you can create, and these are as follows:

  Full Backup
  This the most basic and comprehensive backup method, where all data is copied and sent to another location.

  Incremental Backup
  This method backs up all files that have changed since the last backup occurred, whether it was a Full Backup or a Differential one.

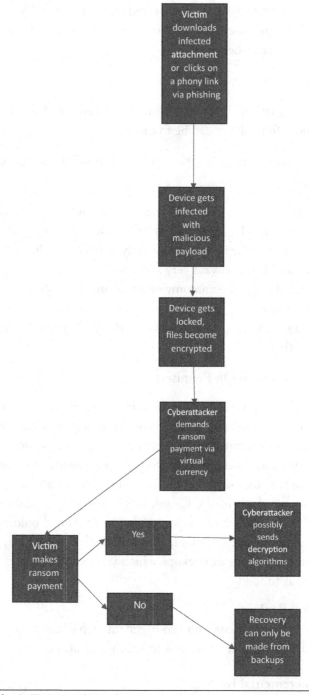

Figure 1.1   An illustration of how a Ransomware attack is launched.

Differential Backup

This method backs up only copies of all files that have changed since the last Full Backup.

It should also be noted that there are advantages and disadvantages to all three methods, and they are as follows:

For the Full Backup
The Advantages

- A very quick restoration time.
- Storage capacity and management is efficient since all the data is stored in a single version.
- You can implement a very easy version control system that allows you to maintain and restore different versions.
- Searching for even the most granular of files is extremely easy.

The Disadvantages

- It demands the most storage space and capacity and management.
- Depending on the size of your datasets, it can take a long time to back up all of your files.
- This can be the most expensive backup method.
- The risk of data loss is high since all the data is stored in one central location.

For the Incremental Backup
The Advantages

- Very efficient use of storage space since files are not replicated in their entirety.
- You can create very quick and fast backups.
- This kind of methodology can be initiated and executed as often as desired, with each increment being an individual recovery point.

The Disadvantages

- The data restoration can be very time-consuming since the datasets must be pieced together from multiple backups.

- Any successful data recovery is only possible if all the backup files are damage-proof and have remained intact.
- The data file search is extremely cumbersome – you need to scout through more than one backup set to restore a specific file.

For the Differential Backup
The Advantages

- It takes less space than creating Full Backups.
- You will experience faster restoration times when compared to Incremental Backups.

The Disadvantages

- There is the potential for a failed recovery if any of the backup sets are incomplete.
- When compared to Incremental Backups, this backup methodology takes longer and requires much more storage space.
- When compared to the other two backup methodologies just examined, the restoration process is slow and complex.

The question that often gets asked at this point, is what kind of backup regime should you observe and practice? Well, a lot of that depends upon your own security requirements. It would probably be best to do at least one Full Backup and at least one Incremental Backup or Differential Backup on a weekly basis.

But it is important to note that On Premises backups like these can be expensive, because extra staffing is needed to do them. However, there is another alternative to this, which is probably far superior – doing backups in the Cloud.

2) Create Backups in the Cloud:
The last subsection reviewed the different types of backups that can be done On Premises, as well as the advantages and disadvantages of all three methodologies. Although these have been the traditional ways of doing backups, not only are they expensive to do and maintain, but they can also pose a grave

security risk, especially to an insider attack, which is so difficult these days to track down. But now, there is an alternative to the traditional On Premises backup – this is creating your backups in the Cloud. This is very easy, and all you need to do is get an account with one of the major Cloud providers, such as the Google Cloud Platform (also known as the GCP), Amazon Web Services (also known as AWS), or Microsoft Azure. The backup tools come with each Cloud subscription that you get, as well as many security features that you can deploy. Here are some of the advantages that the Cloud backup methodology brings to the table:

- It provides an additional location for an off-site data protection in the event of a security breach:
  Any kind of cloud based backup system creates a backup of all the files stored by the business, in which the files are stored in a safe, remote location. This can be very easily retrieved at any time via an Internet connection.
- It is extremely safe and secure:
  Once the data is stored and backed up on a Cloud based platform, it is distributed across redundant servers, safeguarding the data against any kind or type of hardware failures. Also, as an added bonus, automated backups and snapshots are used to ensure further data safety and that the backups are done on a regular schedule.
- It is fully automated:
  Storing and processing data in the Cloud allows you to schedule the backups so they do not interfere with daily business operations. Cloud backup also fully eliminates the need for backing up data manually on a daily basis. For example, you merely select what you want to back up and when and execute it. From there, the Cloud takes care of the rest.
- It is affordable and cost effective:
  You can greatly reduce both your operating and bandwidth costs by switching to a cloud based backup system. You will not be required to procure internal power and resources to store or maintain data remotely. The costs that are associated with the Cloud are fixed, predictable, monthly, and are considered to be an "operational expense" (also known as "OpEx" for short).

- It is easy, accessible, and reliable:
  Cloud based backups do not require any more time commitments from you. Datasets are backed up to the Cloud automatically and on a real-time basis whenever you are connected to the Internet. For example, you can easily drag and drop files into the Cloud. As a result, cloud based backup solutions have made Continuous Monitoring and restoration easy on a 24x7x365 basis.
- A plethora of security features:
  Cloud based backup products and/or services offer a wide range of options and features to keep data safe.
- Easy management:
  Using the Cloud as a means of backup takes far less time and effort than doing On Premises backups.
- Simpler disaster recovery:
  If your business ever experiences a security breach, you can easily roll over to a Cloud based Disaster Recovery as a Service (also known as a "DRaaS"). This option provides disaster recovery services at a fraction of the cost of an On Premises solution.
- You can restore data and very fast:
  If and when a disaster strikes, you cannot afford to wait for hours to recover your data. Simply put, your business cannot afford the cost of downtime, lost revenue, and brand/reputation damage. Since the Cloud can back up services immediately, you can also restore that data rapidly, which can be done within minutes. A reputable cloud based backup system should also help protect against data corruption, one of the most common causes of data loss and data exfiltration. You should also have control over how much bandwidth you need during any specified time, so that you can plan and manage your workload and backup procedures.
- Let your Cloud provider manage the regulatory compliance requirements:
  Today, compliance with the data privacy laws is a must for most businesses. For example, in healthcare, regulations require patient information confidentiality.

But if a practitioner places the backup media containing patient information and data in an unsecure location, the datasets can be exposed to theft and/or exfiltration. A huge advantage of using Cloud based backup services is that you automatically move your data off site to a secure facility – a requirement for many of the regulations, such as the GDPR, CCPA, HIPAA, etc. A Cloud based backup service will also allow you to activate and control the archiving features to help ensure compliance with the regulatory rules of data privacy laws.

- It is "set-it-and-forget it":
Traditional tape recovery methods can take a lot of time. But you cannot afford to lose access to critical data, not even for hours. For example, you can choose which backup functions and features should happen automatically and, at the same time, keep the ability to manage your entire backup and recovery process anywhere and anytime.

- It is highly scalable:
It is a known fact that Cloud based storage is highly scalable and flexible. For example, you can upgrade the service plan whenever you need to, if your security requirements change. If you need to get extra space, it will be added to your subscription.

- It reduces maintenance costs:
As a result of using a cloud based backup system, you will be able to gain access to a modern, high-tech infrastructure to store your datasets. Additionally, you do not have to worry about the maintenance since your Cloud provider will keep a check on upgrades and other technical needs.

- You will have the ability to access your files via the Internet:
If you work remotely, even thousands of miles away, you can still access and restore your data, as long as you have a solid Internet connection. This is in sharp contrast to using an On Premises backup solution, where you have to be physically nearby.

- You can replicate data from multiple sources:
Cloud backups replicate your data across multiple sources, from all over the world, no matter what the file extension

types are. Thus, this further enhances your ability to restore any lost files from their replicated copies. Taken to an extreme, if something should happen to the data center that holds your data, you can restore it from another data center that also hosts said data.

- Backups are fully encrypted:
  Your Cloud provider will most likely be making use of 128-bit encryption to scramble your backups. The key advantage here is that should you become a victim of data exfiltration, there is not much that the cyberattacker can do with the datasets unless they have the decryption algorithms.
- Automatic syncing:
  Another great feature of using a Cloud based backup service is that you can even back up materials as you are working on them. A prime example of this is OneDrive from Microsoft. As you are typing your document in Word, it will automatically back it up in the Cloud at pre-timed intervals.

Finally, for more details on using the Cloud as a backup service, we have published a book entitled *Protecting Information Assets and IT Infrastructure in the Cloud*, second edition. It can be found at:

www.routledge.com/Protecting-In-formation-Assets-and-IT-Infrastructure-in/Das/p/book/9781032605401

The Dark Web

So far in this chapter, we have reviewed how ransomware has evolved from phishing as well as some of the many actions that can be taken to mitigate the chances of becoming a victim of it. Ransomware has evolved to be one of the "uglier" forms of phishing and has even proliferated into a new form of it, which will be examined in the next subsection of this chapter. However, there is yet another huge cyberthreat that still lurks out there, and although it is not a direct form of phishing, it still plays a huge part in its continued evolvement. This is technically known as the "Dark Web", something which most of us have heard about. Yet it still remains a mystery to most, and is still very often confused with the Internet that we visit on a daily basis.

Here is a technical definition of what the Dark Web is all about:

The dark web is the hidden collective of internet sites only accessible by a specialized web browser. It is used for keeping internet activity anonymous and private, which can be helpful in both legal and illegal applications. While some use it to evade government censorship, it has also been known to be utilized for highly illegal activity.[2]

So as you can see, in simpler terms, the Dark Web is a place that a lot of us do not see because, in fact, it takes a specialized web browser to even be able to access it. Because of its covert nature, the Dark Web has now become a place where all sorts of criminal activity takes place, given how inaccessible it is to the general public. But there is more than just one kind of Internet that is available, which is now reviewed.

The Deep Web
The remainder comes from what is known as the "Deep Web" (at 90%), and only a small portion of that actually consists of the Dark Web (6%).

One of the key distinctions between the World Wide Web and the Deep Web is that, with the former, all of the 1.7 billion websites and their corresponding content are known as "indexable". This means that, on a 24x7x365 basis, the search engines of Google, Yahoo, Bing, AOL, etc. are constantly ranking both current and new websites based upon both the search engine optimization (SEO) and the keywords that have been implemented into their respective content.

The end result of all this is that is when you conduct a certain web based query, only the most relevant results will be displayed instantly, just within the first one or two pages of the search results. There will of course be others as well, but they will be filtered based upon their level of relevance in subsequent search page results.

But with the Deep Web, none of the websites and their corresponding pages are indexed. That is one of the major reasons why they are not made available to the public. The terms Dark Web and Deep Web are often used interchangeably, but in reality, the two are actually very different.

The Deep Web is what can be deemed to be "neutral". In other words, it just consists of websites and resources that have been established by entities that do not want their material to be accessed by the public, and out of plain view. Some good examples of this include the federal government and organizations in the healthcare industry, as well as other research and development entities. There is nothing illegal in accessing this part of the Internet. Some of the other key differences between the Deep Web and the Dark Web Internet are as follows:

- The Deep Web is also known as the "Invisible Academic" for reasons just stated.
- Most of the domain extensions in the Deep Web are those of ".onion" and ".12p", very unlike the traditional ".com" domain extensions used by the public Internet.
- The data size of the Deep Web is currently estimated to be 7,500 terabytes. It only consists of about 200,000 websites, but has more than 500X the information and data that the public Internet currently possesses.
- In order to conduct transactions on the Deep Web, only virtual currencies are used, such as Bitcoin.

The Dark Web
Now with the Dark Web, this is considered to be the much more "sinister side" of the Deep Web. For example, this is where most of the illegal activities take place, as well as all of the criminal based chat and messaging forums. In fact, after a cyberattacker has launched their threat vectors, all of the valuable Personally Identifiable Information (PII) datasets that are hijacked eventually make their way down here, so that they can be sold for a profit, or even be used to launch subsequent cyberattacks. Other illegal activities that take place on the Dark Web include the following:

- It is a dumping ground for other confidential information that is stolen, which includes primarily credit card numbers and other relevant banking/financial data.
- It provides the ability to obtain other types of payment cards, forged with stolen credit card numbers.
- How-to guides are available on how to extort and defraud just about any business in virtually all sorts of industries.

- The source code that is leaked from a threat variant (such as that from an SQL injection attack) often makes its way here as well. This allows even the competitors of a business to take complete advantage of this for their own nefarious purposes.
- There are ready made phishing templates and other illegal forms of documentation which guide the cyberattacker in launching a security breach quickly and easily.
- Much more nefarious planning activities take place here as well, especially relating to human trafficking.
- There are already prefilled tax returns with real and legitimate taxpayer information so that the cyberattacker can file fraudulent tax returns in order to get any refunds.
- Fake passes (such as fictitious passports, driver's licenses, military based IDs) are also available here so that a cyberattacker can launch a social engineering attack in a very sophisticated way.

There is much more that goes on; this is only a part of it. Now, the next question comes: Although the Dark Web is the place for all the nasty and illegal stuff to happen, is it still illegal to access it?. Technically, no it is not. But it all comes down to what kind of activities you are doing on the Dark Web. Obviously, if you are engaging in some sort of criminal activity, then yes, this is obviously illegal. But if you are simply going down into the Dark Web to see what it is like, then no, this is not illegal.

In fact, many law enforcement agencies and even IT security teams across corporate America routinely access the Dark Web in order to collect pieces of evidence to build a case for subsequent prosecution and arrests; and the latter penetrates the Dark Web in order to make sure that there are no hijacked PII datasets in it. If there is, then this is the first obvious sign that an organization has been covertly breached by a cyberattacker.

In the next subsection, we give you an overview of how the Dark Web can be accessed.

The Challenges for Law Enforcement on the Dark Web

While policing the public Internet can be a relatively complex task, this is compounded even more in the Dark Web, given the high degree of complexity that is involved. While there are many obstacles involved, the following matrix provides an overview of just what some of the challenges are that law enforcement officials and even digital forensics investigators face when trying to collect evidence on the Dark Web:

THE CHALLENGE	WHY IT IS SO
Higher levels of encryption	There is more of this on the Dark Web than the public Internet. Because of this, it can be almost impossible to keep track of a user's identity, geophysical location, or even what their specific activities are.
High levels of anonymity	Criminals and cyberattackers on the Dark Web, and even legitimate users, try to keep their identity a secret – thus making it difficult to keep track of them.
User identities keep changing	The criminals and cyberattackers on the Dark Web are constantly changing their identities – thus, it is very difficult for law enforcement officials and digital forensics experts to build up reliable profiles on these individuals and/or groups.
The difficulties of jurisdiction	Traditionally, law enforcement is done in the jurisdiction in which it happens. But on the Dark Web, with everything being hidden, especially the geophysical location, it is nearly impossible to determine which law enforcement agency has control over what. Thus, this could make the collectability and preservation of evidence even more questionable.
It takes highly skilled professionals	Trying to track criminals and cyberattackers on the Dark Web requires that the law enforcement official get into the actual mindset of them. The only way to truly do this is to hire people who have turned from the "bad side" to the "good side" – but in the end, how trustworthy can they really be?
Evidence collected comes in different formats	Once a digital forensics team gets involved collecting evidence on the Dark Web, one of the key challenges that arises is that there is no set of best standards or practices which allows for it to be admissible in a court of law without any question.

THE CHALLENGE	WHY IT IS SO
Tracebacking becomes more difficult	This is the process where any type or kind of illicit activities or transactions can be traced back to their source. While this may be a relatively easy task to do on the public Internet, because of the availability of resources this is far more difficult to do on the Dark Web.

There are also difficulties that law enforcement can have even when collecting evidence. Here is a sampling. But first, latent evidence can be technically defined as follows:

> The word latent implies that the prints are hidden or not easily seen without help (either chemical, physical, photographic, or electronic development).[3]

- Very small pieces of digital evidence such as Bitcoins, are very difficult to track down. But they are needed, as they can be linked to other, much larger pieces of latent evidence.
- Because the cyberattacker now uses a myriad of sophisticated tools when they are in the Dark Web, it is very difficult for experts to build a comprehensive profile on them.
- Trying to prove the authenticity of digital evidence that is "anonymized" can prove to be a very laborious process, with no guarantees that it would be admissible in a court of law, if even the most minute trace of legitimacy can be ascertained.
- As mentioned, just about everything on the Dark Web is encrypted to some degree or another. As a result, this makes it that much more difficult to capture any digital evidence on a real-time basis. The only way this can be done is by actually "jailbreaking" into the physical RAM of the server that is hosting a targeted website in order to collect this kind of evidence, while still maintaining its integrity at the same time.
- It is very difficult for digital forensics investigators and law enforcement officials to actually break into a particular device in order to collect evidence. This is best exemplified by Apple and the FBI. In a number of instances, the FBI could not break into the security features of the iPhone, and Apple refused

to cooperate and help in this regard. Their claim was that it would invade not only the privacy rights of the individual in question but would also give away their trade secrets when it came to their encryption algorithms.

- The various marketplaces on the Dark Web in which illicit transactions take place are very often hardened. Thus, this makes it even more difficult to collect any latent pieces of digital evidence.
- Once one piece of digital evidence has been found, it is often difficult to find other pieces that relate to it, thus making it even harder to build a case against an alleged perpetrator.
- The use of cryptocurrencies often hinders the process of tracking down a cyberattacker. For example, they could use the Bitcoin in one marketplace, but use an entirely different currency in another marketplace.

Now that we have provided an overview of what it takes to get into the Dark Web, here is now a review of what you can actually find down there.

The Available Resources Worth Taking a Look at

On the public Internet, while freedom of speech and expression for the most part is protected, there are certain geographic regions around the world where this is strictly forbidden. Therefore, there are many individuals, and even business entities, that create specialized forums and websites so that they can express their views freely, without the fear of censorship.

In a way, this can be considered a good aspect of the Dark Web. But even then, one still has to be careful, because even a website and/or forum that has been created with good intentions can still be spoofed into a malicious one. So, in this regard, here some other websites that are available for accessing and viewing on the Dark Web:

1) Facebook:
   Believe it or not, there is another version of this that lurks down there. One can create an anonymous account in order to help protect one's identity. But given how stealthy people

are on the Dark Web, this probably will not last for too long. This "other version" of Facebook has been created for the sole purpose of avoiding censorship, as just discussed.

2) The haven for Bitcoins:

People very often have the notion that the Bitcoin and other virtual currencies are relatively new. While this may be true on the public Internet, it is far from true on the Dark Web. They have been in existence for many years and these are what are used to conduct financial transactions. The reason for this is simple: You never want to pay with a credit card, check, or even cash on the Dark Web. Not only is this the prime way to steal your identity, but law enforcement will have a much easier time in tracking your movements. By paying with a virtual currency, your anonymity remains relatively intact.

3) BBC News:

This famous news outlet also has its own website on the Dark Web as well. The idea here is to also avoid censorship in those countries where it is banned. Here, people can freely access news stories, and share thoughts, ideas, and comments. The news is not just restricted to what is happening in the United Kingdom, it covers events that happen on a global basis.

4) A place for investigative journalism:

Probably one of the more famous portals for this is known as "ProPublica", as it maintains a rather strong presence on the public Internet as well. In this regard, investigative journalism can thrive as much as it can, because with being on the Dark Web, people and groups can pretty much post anything they want to, or even provide evidence for an ongoing investigative story. Another news portal that is similar in this regard is known as "SecureDrop". This is a specific place witnesses (aka "whistleblowers") can meet with investigative journalists in order to share what they know while still remaining anonymous. In fact, some of the largest news entities have even formed their own SecureDrop websites on the Dark Web, and examples of this include the following:

• Forbes.
• Reuters.
• The Financial Times.

The Communication Services

Yes, there are even various modes of communication on the Dark Web. Probably one of the most favored ones is that of posting on forums. But there is no guarantee of anonymity here. So, in an effort to do this, various email services have emerged. A sampling of these are as follows:

1) Proton Mail:

   This is an email software package that was actually developed in Switzerland. This has been deemed to be one of the most robust and secure email services that is available for use on the Dark Web. In fact, if you set up an account with them, you do not have to provide any sort of personal or confidential information about yourself. It has been designed to work in conjunction with the Tor Web Browser (which was reviewed in detail in the last white paper), thus making it more difficult for people to track your movements on the Dark Web – but keep in mind that there is no guarantee in this either.

2) SecMail:

   This is another email service that is almost as popular as Proton Mail. The only drawback here is that you are allocated only 25 MB of storage space.

3) ZeroBin:

   This email package has been designed specifically for the Dark Web, but it also contains a chatting mechanism as well. What is nice about this is that after you have copied and pasted any content, it gets automatically encrypted; and the content of your email/chat message can also be protected with any type of password that you choose to create (of course, if it is long with alphanumeric values, the better it will be).

Now, here is where phishing and the Dark Web come together. Now that you have seen all of the intricacies of the Dark Web and just how elusive it can be, it is a highly favored place in which the cyberattacker can sell all of the information and data that they have stolen in a phishing attack.

Some common examples include:

- Phishing attacks.
- Exploiting vulnerabilities in a system.
- "Piggybacking".[4]

We reviewed ransomware in quite a bit of detail in the last subsection, but the cyberattacker can now resort to a newer method of attack, which is technically known as "Ransomware as a Service", or "RaaS" for short. It can be defined as follows:

> Ransomware as a service (RaaS) is a malicious adaptation of the software as a service (SaaS) business model. It is a subscription-based model that sells or rents predeveloped ransomware tools to buyers, called ransomware affiliates, to execute ransomware attacks.[5]

So, as described in this definition, RaaS is a subscription based service which a cyberattacker can literally rent out for a very cheap cost. In turn, the owners of the RaaS service will launch the ransomware attack. Or on the other hand, they can also create a malicious payload (the malware) and the cyberattacker can rent that out as well to launch their brand of ransomware attacks.

But as technology has evolved recently, many cybervendors are now offering a specialized kind of Vulnerability Scan that can check for any of your PII datasets. Here are some of the details on how this process can be accomplished:

It is important to note at this point that the terms "Dark Web Monitoring" and "Dark Web Scanning" are very often used synonymously. However, the two are very different in their meaning. The former refers to monitoring the Dark Web on a regular and frequent basis, whereas the latter refers to doing just a one-off dive into the Dark Web. In order to keep your company well protected, it is therefore highly recommended that your IT security team engage in active and frequent monitoring.

There is also confusion about whether Dark Web Monitoring also involves penetration testing. Truth be told, it does not. The primary reason for this is that there are many parts of it that are still sealed off, and when you do a deep dive into it, you want to keep your identity secret as much as possible. Also, keep in mind that penetration testing can often take quite some time to accomplish, and when you are in the Dark Web, you want to stay for as little time as possible so that your IT security team cannot be tracked down.

Therefore, the primary activities that you will be engaged in for the most part will be visiting and monitoring the various forums and online stores where any stolen PII datasets are often bought and sold.

The Benefits of Dark Web Scanning

There are other benefits to conducting Dark Web Monitoring exercises, and these include the following:

1) Cutting down on any further damage:
   The trend today is for the cyberattacker to take a long time to study the profiles of their intended victims. They do this in order to determine the most vulnerable point at which they can penetrate covertly. Once in, the goal is to stay in for as long as possible and move in a lateral fashion so that other areas of the IT/network infrastructure can be entered into as well. The PII datasets are not going to be stolen in one huge swipe; rather, they will be taken out bit by bit so that your IT security team does not notice until is too late. But if you engage in routine monitoring of the Dark Web, and if by chance you come across any information/data that looks like it was stolen from your company, this will be your first indication that a cyberattacker has entered into your system. From here, you can then take actions to kick them out of your IT/network infrastructure and seal off any holes that are still lurking (this is where a penetration test can be used in conjunction with the Dark Web Monitoring exercise). Of course, the sooner you do this, the better, before the real damage starts to set in for your company.

2) Beefing up your lines of defense:
   The common thinking here is that by merely conducting a Cyber Risk Analysis you will then know exactly the steps that you need to take to make your defense perimeter even stronger. While this is certainly true to an extent, engaging in

Dark Web Monitoring can also help you to further pinpoint those areas in defense mechanisms that still need more work. For example, once you know that some of your PII datasets have actually found their way onto the Dark Web, your IT security team can then backtrack to determine the manner in which they were actually stolen. From there, you will then be able to determine where the weak spot was. For example, even though your databases may have been upgraded with the latest patches and upgrades, there could have been a security flaw in the source code which allowed the cyberattacker to penetrate into and covertly hijack this information.

3) Coming into compliance:

With the advent of the remote workforce now taking a permanent hold, it is expected that both the GDPR and the CCPA will now be strictly enforced. A major part of these key pieces of legislation is making sure that the PII datasets that are housed in your database are protected by the best layers of defense possible. By demonstrating this to regulators, you can prove to them that you are taking a proactive stance in taking further steps to protect these mission critical pieces of information and data, if you are ever audited. Also, by engaging in this kind of activity now, you will be able to quickly implement the right controls before it is too late if your IT security team does discover any corporate information/data for sale on the Dark Web.

Extortion Style Attacks

So far in this chapter, we have reviewed not only what phishing is all about, but also two of the three extreme variants of it: Ransomware, and the selling of PII datasets on the Dark Web. This is also known as "data exfiltration", and it is commonly done these days during a phishing attack. But there now exists another worst-case scenario, which is known as "extortion". Most of us are probably familiar with this term, but it can be technically defined as follows:

Extortion is the wrongful use of actual or threatened force, violence, or intimidation to gain money or property from an individual or entity. Extortion generally involves a threat being made to the victim's person or property, or to their family or friends.[6]

So, as you can see, extortion will usually happen if a cyberattacker threatens to reveal something about you to the public unless you pay them a certain amount of money. Typically, this happens after you have become a victim of a ransomware attack. Of course, nobody wants to have their private and confidential information/data revealed to the public, so it would be quite tempting to pay up the money and have nothing ever happen to you. But this is very analogous to the question what we posed earlier in this chapter: Should you pay the ransom after a ransomware attack? In the case of extortion attacks, a situation may even arise where the cyberattacker really has no material against you and is just trying to scare you into giving them money. He or she is merely going on the *assumption that you think they have something of yours.* But the bottom line here is that this is the new wave of phishing attacks that are occurring, and it is becoming worse all the time. Another issue compounding this is the quick evolution of Generative AI, and this will be discussed in the next section of this chapter.

The Multi-Extortion Attack

It is important to note that extortion that has stemmed from a ransomware attack simply does not have to stop at just one instance. In fact, the new trend now is to launch multiple rounds of them. This is technically known as "multi-extortion ransomware". It can be defined as follows:

> Multi-extortion ransomware, sometimes called multifaceted extortion, uses multiple layers of attack to persuade victims to pay a ransom to the attacker. In addition to encrypting files, this type of cybersecurity attack might include additional attack methods, such as file exfiltration, distributed denial of service (DDoS) attacks or extending ransoms to third-party associates.[7]

The Double Extortion Attack

Double extortion ransomware adds a second layer to the ransomware attack. As previously mentioned, this involves data exfiltration files and threatening to publicly release your data unless you pay the ransom. This added threat increases the pressure on the victim to pay the ransom quickly before anything nefarious happens.

Double extortion ransomware attacks can be very damaging because they can totally disrupt your ability to access your own data while also exposing sensitive or confidential information to the public.

The Triple Extortion Attack

As the title implies, triple extortion ransomware attacks involve one more layer of attack on top of the other two (which are file encryption and data theft), as mentioned in the last subsection. Depending on the type of ransomware variant, this could take many forms. For example, it could involve a service disruption to critical infrastructure via a Distributed Denial of Service (DDoS) attack. Or your business could experience a threat to your mission critical operations.

The Quadruple Extortion Attack

A fourth attack layer is what is known as a "third party associate" attack. This is where the cyberattacker threatens and demands ransom payments to be made from you to the original clients, suppliers, or other key stakeholders.

Summarizing the Extortion Attacks

Here are the four attacks, in summary format:

- Single Layer Extortion:
  This is deemed to be the first multi-extortion ransomware phase that totally involves encryption. Attackers either encrypt whole systems or select files that are deemed to be highly important.
- Double Layer Extortion:
  In this particular instance, the cyberattacker has added another phase of extortion, that involves data exfiltration, which has become very popular because of malware such as Maze and DoppelPaymer.

- Third Layer Extortion:
A triple extortion attack can take different forms, but it greatly expands the playing field further for the cyberattacker. As mentioned, the cyberattacker might use a service disruption attack to apply further and graver pressure. The AvosLocker malware is commonly used in this regard.
- Fourth Layer Extortion:
As previously described, this involves your third party contacts. A prime example of this is the Quanta security breach. When they failed to pay the REvil ransomware group, the cyberattackers turned towards extorting Apple, one of Quanta's key clients.
- Fifth Layer Extortion:
This is yet another ransomware extortion tactic, which was first used by the DarkSide ransomware group. This is where publicly traded companies are threatened by offering short stock opportunities to unscrupulous financial traders. In this type of cyberattack, threats are made to publicly list the victim organization's name, with the end result being that the stock price will fall. With insider knowledge of this, a financial trader could stand to make a rather large profit.

These are all illustrated in Figure 1.2:

The Rise of Artificial Intelligence in Phishing

Up to this point in this chapter, to summarize we have reviewed what phishing is, how it has evolved, and some of the worst threat variants which include the following:

- Ransomware.
- Data exfiltration onto the Dark Web.
- Ransomware extortion attacks.

But there is a new trend now which is going to greatly impact how phishing attacks will be launched. This is the emergence of Artificial Intelligence, also known much more commonly as "AI". It can be technically defined as follows:

Figure 1.2 Diagram of the different kinds of Extortion attacks.

Artificial intelligence, or AI, is technology that enables computers and machines to simulate human intelligence and problem-solving capabilities.[8]

In simpler terms, AI tries to mimic the thought and reasoning processes of the human brain. But it is very important to keep in mind here that *we will never even come close to a 0.5% understanding of what the human brain is truly all about.*

In general, AI is powered by algorithms. These are merely the mathematical representations of how the human brain possibly works. In turn, it is these algorithms which constitute what is known as the "AI model". This can also be technically defined as follows:

> An AI model is a program that has been trained on a set of data to recognize certain patterns or make certain decisions without further human intervention.[9]

So, think of the AI model as a total representation of the human brain, and the algorithms as the "neurons".

But in order to fully drive the AI model and the algorithms, data is needed, and lots of it. This is reviewed in the next subsection.

The Importance of Data

Our next chapter will review this in much more detail. But for the purposes of this chapter, an AI model can be fed or "ingested" (this is the technical term) two types of data:

1) Structured Data:
   Think of an Excel spreadsheet with columns and rows, filled with all kinds of numbers. This is also referred to as "quantitative data". This is the perfect example of a structured dataset being fed into an AI model.

2) Unstructured Data:
   Unlike an Excel spreadsheet as just described, unstructured data can take on different formats, such as photos, images, videos, etc. This is also referred to as "qualitative data".

So, in the end, an AI model is fed all of this data (whether it is quantitative or qualitative, or even both) in order for it to "learn".

The ultimate goal of the entire AI system is to generate an "output" that answers a specific query that you ask of it.

We have covered a lot of concepts up this point, so the illustration here (Figure 1.3) summarizes all of this.

Figure 1.3   Illustration of how an AI Model works.

A very good example of this is ChatGPT. This is an AI system that was designed to answer queries of all types and kinds. It was developed by OpenAI and is hosted primarily on Microsoft Azure. You can either type in or even submit your query via voice. From there, ChatGPT will then search through all of the datasets that it has been trained on, and it will then provide an answer to you. For example, if you ask it to find a choice of good restaurants, it will search through its datasets to tell you what will be best for your appetite.

The Dangers of Artificial Intelligence in Phishing

It should be noted that although AI has a tremendous amount of potential, it does have its "dark side" as well. Meaning, it can be used to create email messages that look so real and convincing that it is almost impossible to tell a fake email from a legitimate one. Here are some ways in which an AI-based phishing attack can take place:

1) Data Harvesting:
   The Cyberattacker can collect extensive datasets about you through social media profiles, job titles, email addresses, and more, using OSINT tools (Open Source Intelligence).
2) Email Content Generation:
   AI algorithms can tailor an email message to appear as if it is coming from a trusted source, such as a colleague, a boss, a coworker, or even a legitimate organization.
3) Behavioral Analysis:
   AI-driven algorithms tools can adapt and evolve by analyzing end user behavior. For example, if somebody opens an email, downloads an attachment, or clicks on the links, the AI algorithms can take all of this into account to fine tune future phishing attempts.
4) Contextual Deception:
   AI-based phishing emails can include relevant information about you to increase apparent authenticity. For example, they may reference recent events or specific projects that you took part in at your place of employment.

5) Avoidance of Detection:

AI-based phishing attacks can bypass traditional email security filters (such as anti-malware and anti-virus software packages) by evading keyword based detection systems. As a result, they can generate unique, non-standard content that will not trigger alarm bells.

6) Credential Theft:

The ultimate goal of AI phishing attacks is to trick individuals in a very convincing way into revealing sensitive information, primarily their passwords.

7) Vishing:

This is an acronym for "voice phishing" This is where AI is used to create fake phone calls, voice messages, and voicemails to trick people into sharing their sensitive information.

8) Spear Phishing:

This is where AI is used to create an email message about an event that just recently happened to you. For example, if you visit a specific hospital, an AI model can send you an email claiming to be that hospital needing to verify your account information to pay for a bill. This is used to trick you into handing over your credit card information to a cyberattacker. They can now train an AI model to do it for them, quickly and automatically.

9) Creation of Deepfakes:

With AI, the cyberattacker can create realistic audio and video content that impersonates individuals or organizations. This manipulative technique can be extremely deceptive and is often used in elections, to trick voters into donating money through a phony website.

10) Creation of Chatbots:

AI-powered chatbots can be used to create very deceptive virtual agents. This allows them to engage with a lot of targets at one time, reaching more targets than with traditional phishing methods. Even worse, chatbots can be programmed to initiate conversations with people and convince them to provide sensitive information or click on malicious links. They can become more sophisticated over time, making them harder to detect.

An example of how AI-generated phishing emails are used in the healthcare sector can be found at: http://cyberresources.solutions/GenAI_Book/AI_Phishing.pdf

The Evolution of Generative AI

The latest trend in AI today is what is known as "Generative AI". This is a term that is commonly associated with ChatGPT, but there is still a great deal of confusion as to what it is all about. It can be technically defined as follows:

> Generative AI is a type of artificial intelligence technology that can produce various types of content, including text, imagery, audio and synthetic data.[10]

But Generative AI is distinct from the traditional AI models discussed throughout this chapter from three perspectives:

- Generative AI models can create outputs that are unique, but above all fresh. For example, traditional AI models can only produce output based upon the datasets that they have been trained on and datasets that are fed into them on a real-time basis. This is also viewed as "Garbage In, Garbage Out". In other words, you get only what you input into the AI model. But with Generative AI, it takes this one step further. Depending on what you ask it to do via the query, an AI model like ChatGPT can actually *search for outside sources of information on it, which are totally independent from the datasets that it has been trained on.*
- Generative AI makes heavy usage of another field called "Prompt Engineering". A technical definition of this is as follows:
  Prompt engineering is the process where you guide generative artificial intelligence (generative AI) solutions to generate desired outputs. Even though generative AI attempts to mimic humans, it requires detailed instructions to create high-quality and relevant output.[11]

Put in simpler terms, since Generative AI is so much more advanced than the traditional AI models, in order to get the best possible output you need to make your query as specific as possible. This topic will be explained later, in the chapter about Generative AI.

- With the traditional AI models, the output is usually given out in a text format. But with Generative AI, your outputs can come in a wide variety of formats that include text, video, images, and even audio formats, depending upon what you select when you pose your query.

While there are many advantages and benefits of Generative AI, there is also a bad side. And once again, it all comes down to cybersecurity. For example, Generative AI is most suited here for the automation of repetitive tasks, such as those that are found in penetration testing and threat hunting. And Generative AI is also quite beneficial when it comes to filtering out false positives and predicting future threat variants.

But it can also be used for highly nefarious purposes, such as creating the source code for malware (to be used in ransomware attacks), or making phishing emails so sophisticated that it is almost impossible to tell if they are fake or not (as described in the last subsection). Here are some other examples as to how Generative AI can be used for nefarious purposes in cybersecurity:

1) Data Overflow:
   The end user can input any kind of data into Generative AI services via free form text boxes, including sensitive, private, or proprietary information. The perfect example of this is open source software such as APIs. They can contain sensitive data like API keys that give special access to customer information.
2) Web Application Attacks:
   This will come in the form of IP leakages. This is primarily due to the ease of use of web- or app-based AI tools and risks creating another form of shadow IT.
3) The Use of Data in Training:
   Generative AI models need a lot of data and information to learn from, and it is quite possible that data could be highly sensitive. If it is not safeguarded and managed carefully, the

datasets could unintentionally be revealed during training, causing grave privacy issues.

4) The Storage of Data:

It is a known fact that Generative AI models are better optimized with more data. But the data needs to be stored in a safe location while the models learn and improve. This means sensitive datasets will most likely be kept in third party storage spaces, where the potential for misuse, leakage, or exfiltration is quite strong.

5) Data Privacy/Compliance:

With the review of datasets, there is the strong possibility that PII datasets could be highly prone to coming under the scrutinization of data privacy laws, such as GDPR, CCPA, HIPAA, etc.

6) Synthetic Data:

Generative AI models can create synthetic data. A technical definition of it is as follows:

Synthetic data is non-human-created data that mimics real-world data. It is created by computing algorithms and simulations based on generative artificial intelligence technologies.[12]

As a result, this can lead to grave concerns about what is real and fake data, and where it actually originated from. Also, synthetic data could leave behind small pieces of patterns or details that might lead to people being identified in a covert way.

7) Model Poisoning:

This type of threat involves the manipulation of an existing model so that it produces false or misleading results.

8) The Rise of Adversarial Attacks:

This where the cyberattacker manipulates the Generative AI algorithms so that the weaknesses of the models can be fully exploited. A typical example of this is an attack that causes an algorithm to make a mistake or misclassify data.

9) Altering Content:
Generative AI can also alter and manipulate content by changing the meaning or context of words or phrases in any of the generated outputs such as images, text, videos, audio, etc.

10) Novices Launching Attacks:
The wide, easy access to Generative AI tools is further facilitating an automated process for building up a profile on an intended target. This ease of access empowers nonprofessionals to attempt a range of cyberattacks, which they have not done previously.

For the remainder of this book, we will examine closely the "good side" of Generative AI. It is divided as follows:

- Chapter 2: A deeper dive into AI, Neural Networks, and Machine Learning.
- Chapter 3: A more detailed review of Generative AI and the other areas of AI that it is affiliated with.
- Chapter 4: A review of key cybersecurity metrics and Key Performance Indicators (KPIs).
- Chapter 5: A proposed Generative AI model and how it can be used to mitigate the risks of sophisticated phishing attacks happening.

Notes

1 www.ibm.com/topics/ransomware
2 https://usa.kaspersky.com/resource-center/threats/deep-web
3 https://ncdoj.gov/crime-lab/latent-evidence/
4 www.splunk.com/en_us/blog/learn/data-exfiltration.html
5 www.paloaltonetworks.com/cyberpedia/what-is-ransomware-as-a-service
6 www.investopedia.com/terms/e/extortion.asp
7 www.paloaltonetworks.com/cyberpedia/what-is-multi-extortion-ransomware
8 www.ibm.com/topics/artificial-intelligence
9 www.ibm.com/topics/ai-model
10 www.techtarget.com/searchenterpriseai/definition/generative-AI
11 https://aws.amazon.com/what-is/prompt-engineering/
12 https://aws.amazon.com/what-is/synthetic-data/

2

OVERVIEW OF ARTIFICIAL INTELLIGENCE, NEURAL NETWORKS, AND MACHINE LEARNING

An Introduction to Artificial Intelligence

The concept of Artificial Intelligence (AI) is not a new one; it goes back to the late 1960s. While there were some applications being developed at the time for it, it did not really pick up the huge momentum that it has until now, with the advent of ChatGPT. And as we know, anything that is related to AI is now a big buzzword of the industry. Although one of the strongest areas of interest for AI has been cybersecurity, it is also receiving a lot of attention in other areas as well, most especially when it comes to supply chains/logistics.

A big area where it is getting attention is in what is known as "robotic process automation". It can be technically defined as follows:

> Robotic process automation (RPA), also known as software robotics, uses intelligent automation technologies to perform repetitive office tasks of human workers, such as extracting data, filling in forms, moving files and more.[1]

The perfect example of this is in car assembly lines. Today, robotic arms are being used to build car components, paint the sides of cars, etc.

Another great example of the broad usage of AI in any industry is what are known as "digital twins". This is where a virtualized copy of a real-world object is created.

DOI: 10.1201/9781003503781-2

Another good example of this would be the aircraft industry. For example, rather than building an actual physical prototype of a wing, it can be duplicated in a virtual machine, using AI.

There are many advantages to making use of digital twins, some of which include the following:

- Faster time to prototyping.
- Quicker results.
- Various "what if" scenarios can be created without having to build separate, physical mockups.
- It is far cheaper, and actually much more realistic, than what the physical mockups can offer, such as seeing images in three-dimensional views.

But as it relates to cybersecurity, one of the main areas where Artificial Intelligence is playing a key role is in task automation. For instance, both penetration testing and threat hunting are very time consuming, laborious, and mentally grueling exercises for any human being to perform. For example, there are a lot of smaller steps that have to take place in order to yield a good test, and if there are any mistakes made, this could greatly skew the results for the client. As a result, AI can be used here to automate the bulk of these processes, so that the penetration testing/threat hunting teams can stay focused on the bigger picture at hand, as many of these tasks are repetitive. This is where the tools of AI can come into play.

This includes finding both the hidden and unhidden holes and weaknesses in their clients' IT and network infrastructure and providing appropriate courses for remediation.

Another key area in cybersecurity where AI tools are being used is in filtering for false positives. For example, the IT security teams of any business are being totally flooded with warnings and alerts as a result of network security tools such as firewalls, network intrusion devices, and routers. This can be a huge nightmare for a smaller business, as the IT security team would have to manually filter through each one, so that they can be triaged appropriately. This once again is a sheer drain on time and precious resources.

This is where AI can come into play. Assuming that it has been fed the right permutations and inputs, a good AI model should be able to filter out the false positives and present only the real and legitimate ones to the IT security team. This will thus make the triaging process far more efficient and effective, and it will not be a time drain on resources. Very often, the real warnings and alerts can be fed into what is known as "security information and event management" (also known as "SIEM" for short), where they can be presented in a holistic fashion, from a single point of view.

AI can also be used to help businesses conduct a risk assessment study. Essentially, this is where the CISO and the IT security team take an inventory of all of their digital and physical assets. From here their vulnerability is then ranked, for example, on a scale of 1–10, where the value of "1" represents a very minimal risk, and a value of "10" would be maximum risk. Any other values will reflect a higher level of risk, depending upon the asset in question.

So, by using AI for this, not only can the right levels of risk be calculated, but it can also help the business to re-strategize how they deploy their security tools. For example, many organizations today are now starting to realize that having too many security tools to beef up their respective lines of defense is not good at all; in fact, it only increases the attack surface for the cyberattacker.

As an example, rather than deploying ten firewalls, it is far more strategic to deploy perhaps just three where they are needed the most. Also, by taking this kind of mindset, the CISO and their IT security team will achieve a far greater return on investment (ROI), which means that they will be in a much better position to get more money into their cyber budgets.

At this point it is important to define just what exactly Artificial Intelligence is. A technical definition of it is as follows:

> Artificial intelligence (AI) makes it possible for machines to learn from experience, adjust to new inputs and perform human-like tasks. Most AI examples that you hear about today – from chess-playing computers to self-driving cars – rely heavily on deep learning and natural language processing. Using these technologies, computers can be trained to accomplish specific tasks by processing large amounts of data and recognizing patterns in the data.[2]

As one can see from this definition, the main objective of Artificial Intelligence is to have the ability to learn and project into the future by learning from past behaviors. This is heavily dependent upon the datasets that are fed into the AI model in order to derive the desired outputs. One of our previous books, *Practical AI for Cybersecurity*, does a very deep dive into the importance of having optimized datasets. The landing page for this book can be found at:

www.routledge.com/Practical-AI-for-Cybersecurity/Das/p/book/ 9780367437152

The History of Artificial Intelligence

The history of AI is a long one, and is marked by the following events:

1) The development of the Turing Test.
2) The publication of a scientific article entitled "Minds, Brains, and Programs".
3) The publication of a scientific journal article entitled "A Logical Calculus of the Ideas Immanent in Nervous Activity".
4) The Origin Story.
5) Two newer theories on AI.
6) The era of Expert Systems.
7) The evolution of Deep Learning.

The Turing Test

The first well-known figure in the field of Artificial Intelligence is Alan Turing. He is very often referred to as the "Father of Artificial Intelligence". Way back in 1936, he wrote a major scientific paper entitled "On Computable Numbers". In this work, he actually lays down the concepts for what a computer is all about and what its primary purposes are to be.

His basic idea of a computer was based upon the premise that it had to be intelligent in some way and serve a useful purpose. But at this point in time, it was very difficult to come up with an actual measure of what "intelligence" really was. Thus, this gave birth to what is now known as the "Turing Test".

In this scenario, there is a game with three players involved in it. Two of the participants are human beings, and the other is a computer. The third participant is the actual moderator. He or she will ask a series of open-ended questions to both participants, in an effort to determine which of the two of them is actually a human being. If a determination could not be made by asking these open-ended questions, it would then be assumed that the computer could be deemed an "intelligent" entity.

"Minds, Brains, and Programs"

The next major breakthrough after the Turing Test came with the publication of a scientific paper entitled "Minds, Brains, and Programs". This was written by a philosopher called John Searle and was published in 1980. In this research paper, he formulated another model which closely paralleled the Turing Test and which became known as the "Chinese Room Argument".

This paper John Searle wrote also laid down the two types of Artificial Intelligence that could potentially exist:

1) Strong AI:
   This is when a computer truly understands and is fully cognizant of what is transpiring around it. This area of Artificial Intelligence is also technically known as "Artificial General Intelligence", or "AGI" for short.
2) Weak AI:
   This is a form of Artificial Intelligence that is deemed to be not so strong in nature, by being given a very narrow focus or set of tasks to work on.

"A Logical Calculus of the Ideas Immanent in Nervous Activity"

The next major breakthrough to come in Artificial Intelligence was a scientific paper entitled "A Logical Calculus of the Ideas Immanent in Nervous Activity". This was co-written by Warren McCulloch and Walter Pitts in 1943. The major premise of this paper was that logical deductions could explain the powers of the human brain, and it was published in the *Bulletin of Mathematical Biophysics*.

In this paper, McCulloch and Pitts presented the hypothesis that the core functions of the human brain, in particular the neurons and synaptic activities that take place, can be fully explained by mathematical logical operators (for example, And, Not, etc.).

In an effort to build on this, Norbert Wiener created and published an actual scientific book entitled *Cybernetics: Or Control and Communication in the Animal and The Machine*. It introduced a new type of theory called "Chaos Theory". In the book, he also equated the human brain to a computer and said that a computer should be able to play a game of chess. It should be able to learn at even higher planes as it played more games.

The Origin Story

The next major stepping stone in the world of Artificial Intelligence came at Dartmouth College. There was a publication entitled *The Study of Artificial Intelligence*, and this was the first time that this term had ever been used. The exact nature of this project is as follows:

> The study is to proceed on the basis of the conjecture that every aspect of learning or any other feature of intelligence can be [sic] in principle be so precisely described that a machine can be made to simulate it. An attempt will thus be made to find out how to make machines use language, form abstractions and concepts, solve kinds of problems now reserved for humans, and improve themselves. We think that a significant advance can be made in one or more of these problems if a carefully selected group of scientists work on it together for a summer.[3]

During this time frame, a computer program called the "Logic Theorist" was created and developed. The focus of this was to solve complex mathematically based theorems from the publication known as the *Principia Mathematica*. In order to create this programming language, an IBM 701 mainframe computer was also developed, making use of Machine Learning (which will be reviewed further in the next subsection of this chapter).

But in order to further optimize the speed of the "Logic Theorist", a new processing language was used, and this became known as the "Information Processing Language", or "IPL" for short. This led to the creation of yet another development: dynamic memory allocation. As a result, the "Logic Theorist" has been deemed to be the first Artificial Intelligence programming language ever to be created.

Two Newer Theories on AI

Two major theories of Artificial Intelligence also came about, and they are as follows:

1) The need for symbolic systems:
   This would make heavy usage of computer based logic, such as "If–Then–Else" statements.
2) The need for Artificial Intelligence systems to behave more like the human brain:
   This was the first known attempt to map the neurons in the brain, and their corresponding activities. This theory was developed by Frank Rosenblatt, but he renamed the neurons "perceptrons".

Back in 1957, the first Artificial Intelligence application was created, to do this, and it was called the "Mark I Perceptron". The computer that ran this particular program was fitted with two cameras to differentiate two separate images, whose scale was 20x20 pixels. This program would also make use of random based statistical weightings to go through this step-by-step, iterative process:

1) Create and insert an input, but come up with an output that is perceptron based.
2) The input and the output should match, and if they do not, then the following steps should be taken:
   • If the output (the perceptron) was "I" (instead of being 0), the statistical weight for "I" should be decreased.
   • In the reverse of this, if the output (the perceptron) was "I" (instead of being 0), the statistical weight for "I" should be increased by an equal amount.

3) The first two steps should be repeated in a continued, iterative process until "I" = 0, or vice versa.

This AI application also served as the precursor for Neural Networks (which will also be reviewed in this chapter). One of the major flaws of this application is that it only had one layer of processing.

The Era of Expert Systems

During this time frame, there were many other events that took place in the field of Artificial Intelligence. One of these was the development of the backpropagation technique. This is a technique which assigns statistical weights for the inputs that go into a Neural Network system.

Another key development was the creation of what is known as the "Recurrent Neural Network", or "RNN" for short. This technique permits the connections in the Artificial Intelligence system to move seamlessly through both the input and the output layers. Another key catalyst was the evolution of the microcomputer. This led to the development of what are known as "Expert Systems", which made heavy usage of symbolic logic.

One of the best examples of an Expert System was that of the "eXpert CONfigurer", also known as the "XCON" for short. This was developed by John McDermott at Carnegie Mellon University. The main purpose of this was to further advance the computer components, and in the end, the microcomputer developed at that time had about 2,500 rules (both mathematically and statistically based) that were incorporated into it. In a way, this was the forerunner to Virtual Personal Assistants (VPAs) such as Siri and Cortana which allow you to make choices.

The Evolution of Deep Learning

Finally, the 1980s saw the evolution of yet another new era in Artificial Intelligence, known as "Deep Learning".

In simpler terms, this kind of system does not need already established mathematical or statistical algorithms in order to learn from the data that is fed into it. All it needs are certain permutations, and from there it can literally learn on its own and even make projections into the future.

There were also two major developments at this time with regards to Deep Learning:

- In 1980, Kunihiko Fukushima developed an Artificial Intelligence system called the "neocognitron". This was the precursor to the birth of what are known as "Convolutional Neural Networks", or "CNNs" for short. This was based upon the processes that are found in the visual cortex of various kinds of animal.
- In 1982, John Hopfield developed another Artificial Intelligence system called "Hopfield Networks". This laid down the groundwork for what are known as "Recurrent Neural Networks", or "RNNs" for short.

The evolution of AI is illustrated in Figure 2.1:

An Overview of Machine Learning

Although this term is not as widely used as Generative AI, Machine Learning plays a very important role in AI. In fact, it is deemed to be a subset of it, as are Neural Networks (which will be reviewed in more detail in the next subsection), and Computer Vision (this is a branch of AI that tries to replicate the visual process of the human brain). Before we do a deeper dive into what Machine Learning is about, it is first important to give a technical definition of it, which is as follows:

> Machine learning is a subfield of artificial intelligence that gives computers the ability to learn without explicitly being programmed.[4]

It should be noted at this point that when using a traditional AI model, a lot of human intervention is required, not only to ingest the datasets into it but also to help it train over time. From a technical standpoint, this is known as "Supervised Learning". But with Machine Learning (also known as "ML"), human intervention is still required, but only for the initial dataset ingestion.

Figure 2.1   This is how AI has evolved over time.

After that, one of the primary goals of ML is to then have the model train and learn on its own, while at the same time yielding the desired outputs. This is technically known as "Unsupervised Learning".

Apart from these two learning methods, there are also two more which are not used as widely. But nonetheless, it is important to review them at this point. They are as follows:

1) Semi-Structured Learning:

This approach utilizes a hybrid approach of both Supervised and Unsupervised Learning. This is also known as "Self-Supervised Machine Learning". In this instance, human intervention is still required to feed in the datasets into the AI model, but the algorithms can still learn if the datasets are not categorized or classified. Also, with this kind of training, even qualitative based datasets can be used for learning as well (which could include audio, images, video, etc.).

2) Reinforcement Learning:

With this kind of approach, the AI model uses a system of "reward and punishment" in order for it to learn. For example, in these kinds of cases, a point system is used. If the AI model yields the correct outputs, it is awarded a certain numerical value. But if the output is skewed for whatever reason, then this numerical value is reduced by a predetermined amount. This technique can be used to help train Digital People (chatbots with a human like interface) to provide the right answers or course of action in response to queries that have been posed to them.

An illustration of Machine Learning follows.

The Learning Process of Machine Learning

As was mentioned in the last subsection, while the goal of ML is to have it learn as much as it can on its own, there is a process that must be followed so that it can generate the right output. This is as follows:

1) Ordering the Data:

In this first step, you want to make sure that the data is cleaned, optimized, and organized in a logical format as much as possible. If there are noticeable outliers or differences amongst the datasets, then the ML algorithms may recognize this as a legitimate pattern, which is obviously something that you do not want to happen.

2) Picking the Algorithm:
   In this second step, you will want to select the appropriate learning technique, as just reviewed in the last subsection of this chapter. Preference should always be geared towards Unsupervised Learning.
3) Training the Model:
   This is where the learning process for the AI model starts. It will look for various associations and relationships amongst the datasets so that the desired outputs can be formulated.
4) Evaluation of the Model:
   In this fourth step, after the training has been completed, you will then evaluate the results of the output. If they answer the query or the objective, then the training can be deemed to have been successful. If not, you will have to go back and examine if there were any errors in the dataset that was ingested into the AI model.
5) Further Fine Tuning and Optimization:
   The final step will then be to make sure that the AI model is always producing the desired outputs. This is where optimization and fine tuning come into play. Also, this is where you want to have deployed Unsupervised Learning; if not, human intervention will be a huge time and resource drain.

This entire process is illustrated here:

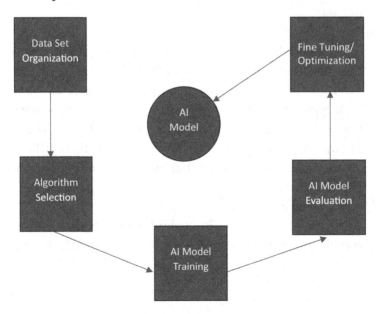

The Machine Learning Algorithms

Now that we have reviewed how the ML process works, it is important to highlight at this point what some of the major algorithms are. They are as follows:

1) The Naïve Bayes Classifier:
   The reason why this algorithm is called "naïve" is that the underlying assumption is that each of the datasets are independent from one another. In other words, the statistical occurrence of one variable in one dataset will have nothing whatsoever to do with the variables in the remaining datasets.

2) The K-Nearest Neighbor:
   This algorithm is used for classifying any dataset or datasets that you have, quantitative or qualitative based, or even both. The basic theoretical construct of this is that those values that are closely related, or associated with one another, in your datasets will statistically be good predictors for an AI model. In order to use this, you need first to compute the numerical distance between the closest values. Next, you will then have to ascertain the total number of values that are closely aligned with another. Remember, to help accommodate this you can always assign higher value statistical weights to those particular values that are closely affiliated with one another amongst the datasets.

3) The Decision Tree:
   This methodology actually provides an alternative to the other two techniques described thus far. In fact, the Decision Tree works far better and much more efficiently with qualitative based datasets. The main starting point of the decision is at the node, which typically starts at the top of any given chart. From this point onwards, there will be a series of decision branches that will be stemming out, thus giving it its name.

4) The Ensemble Model:
   As its name implies, this is a hybrid based algorithm, using a combination of the first three algorithms, in no particular order.

5) The K-Means Clustering:
This methodology is very useful for extremely large datasets, especially those that are termed "Big Data datasets".

The Perceptron

As we know, the central processing unit (CPU) is the main processing component of a computer. But if one were to equate this to the level of the brain, then it is called the "neuron". The human brain consists of many neurons, and according to some scientific studies there are as many as almost 90 billion of them. Research has also shown that a neuron is typically much slower than a CPU in a computer, but this is due to the fact that that there are so many of them, and the connections between the perceptrons are even larger.

These connections are known as "synapses", and interestingly enough, they work in a parallel fashion from one another, much like parallel processing in a computer. It should be noted that in a computer, the CPU is always active and the memory (such as the RAM) is a separate entity. But in the human brain, all of the synapses are actually distributed evenly over its own network, and everything is connected and interlinked with one another.

A perceptron can be technically defined as follows:

Perceptron is a single layer neural network and a multi-layer perceptron is called Neural Networks.[5]

In the next subsection of this chapter, we provide a review of Neural Networks.

An Overview of Neural Networks

The Neuron

Just like Machine Learning (ML), Neural Networks are also deemed to be a subcomponent of AI. The theory behind Neural Networks (NNs) lies around the neuron, which was introduced earlier in this chapter, in the subsection entitled "The Perceptron". As was described, the neuron is considered to be the building block of all of the processes that take place within the human brain.

There are three key concepts that are associated with the neuron, and they are as follows:

1) The Axon:

This is deemed to be the "transmitting" part of the neuron. This action causes the release of neurotransmitters to take place within the human brain.

2) The Spine:

This is not to be confused with the spinal cord. Rather, the spine is made up of protrusions that can be found at the edges of the dendrite and are used as the main point of contact for a neuron to communicate with another neuron.

3) The Dendrite:

This is deemed to be the "receiving end" of the neuron. Dendrites receive the synaptic inputs from the many axons. What is unique about the dendrite is that it is the sum total of inputs that will actually determine if the neuron will be activated or still lie in a dormant state.

4) The Action Potential:

This is electrical activity that will "activate" the neuron to communicate with the other neurons. This stimulation causes the release of the neurotransmitter into the synapse. In turn, this will allow a particular neuron to communicate with other neurons within the human brain.

5) The Synapse:

Although this too was examined earlier in this chapter, this is technically the juncture point between the endings (or "terminals"). From here, the dendrites then connect this neuron with the next one, so that activity can take place. There are two kinds of synapses:

- The Chemical Synapse:

  Any activation is carried along from one axon to the next one via the use of a chemical messenger known as the "neurotransmitter". In turn, the neurotransmitter can stimulate the postsynaptic neurons that generate an action potential.

- The Electrical Synapse:
  When a neuron is connected to another neuron, it is done via a gap junction. Gap junctions consist of ion based channels that assist in the transmission of a positive electrical signal between the two neurons.

6) The Soma:
This is the actual cellular structure of the neuron. It contains the DNA and other organelles like mitochondria, the Golgi apparatus, and the cytoplasm that are associated with the neuron.

7) The Myelin:
This is a substance that surrounds the different sections of the axon, and is used to speed up the transmission between two neurons. There are breaks between the myelin, known as the "nodes of Ranvier". This is a high concentration of voltage-gated ion channels, that also bridges two neurons together.

8) The Glial Cells:
These are the components within the neuron. Their job is to provide both physical and chemical support to the neuron and maintain the structure of it.

It is important to note at this point that there are three different kinds of neurons, which are as follows:

1) The Sensory Neurons:
These are neurons that can detect stimuli from the outside environment and convert them in such a way that they can be transmitted to and understood by other neurons. These external stimuli actually activate these kinds of neurons in the spinal cord as well.

2) The Motor Neurons:
These are the neurons that are located in the central nervous system (also known as the "CNS"), and as their name suggests, they transmit information and data from the brain to the muscles in the human body so that they are activated.

3) The Interneurons:
   These kinds of neurons enable communication with the other neurons (sensory and motor) and pass the electrical signals between them.

The Neural Network

The primary reason for providing such an extensive review of the neuron is that it provides the major building block for what are known as "Neural Networks". As mentioned earlier in this chapter, this is yet another subcomponent of AI, just like Machine Learning is. But. Neural Networks are different. For instance, they too need data ingested into them for them to learn, but rather than taking the "Garbage In, Garbage Out" approach that Machine Learning does, the neurons are implemented so that the AI model (which makes use of the Neural Network) can more or less learn on its own, and can learn from any "mistakes" it may have made in the past. An example of this would be producing an output that did not reach the objective or correctly answer a query that was posed to it.

In fact, it can even be considered that Neural Networks are the forerunner to Generative AI, which will be fully explored in Chapter 3 of this book.

The Artificial Neural Network

In more technical terms, the Neural Network that is deployed in an AI model is more commonly known as an "Artificial Neural Network", or "ANN" for short. The ANN consists of three major components:

1) The Input Layer:
   This is also referred to as the "input layer". This is the first step for the ANN to start learning, and it is at this point that the data ingestion process actually starts.
2) The Hidden Layer:
   This is where the neurons (also referred to technically as "nodes") reside. It is important to note that each neuron is assigned a particular statistical weight, which reflects how the datasets that have been ingested will be used, not only for

training purposes but also in creating the desired output. A simple definition of a statistical weight as it applies to ANNs is as follows:

Weights in a neural network are similar to the synaptic strengths in a biological brain. They are parameters that determine how strongly the output of one neuron influences the input of another. Weights control the impact of one neuron on another. During the training process of a neural network, these weights are adjusted to minimize the error between the predicted output and the actual output.[6]

3) The Output Layer:
This is where the output is given, in response to a query or objective that has been posed to the ANN.

This high level process is illustrated in Figure 2.2:
In fact, the ANN can be further customized in order to meet the requirements of a business or organization. There are seven types of ANN which can be custom created, and their categories are as follows:

1) The Feed Forward:
The premise here is quite simple: They process information and data in one direction until an output is ready. This is deemed to be a linear based approach to calculating an output.
2) The Recurrent Neural Network:
These are also known as "RNNs" and are more complex than the Feed Forward models. For example, they reprocess the outputs that they have generated in order to generate more-accurate future outputs going into the future. As a result, a feedback loop is thus created, technically known as a "recurring process".
3) The Convolutional Neural Network:
These are also known as "CNNs". The algorithms that are involved are far more powerful in nature, because they can process complex images, which can be used for Pattern Recognition at a subsequent point in time. In this case, multiple convolutional layers are created, breaking down the

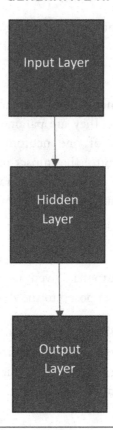

Figure 2.2   These are the components of an ANN.

datasets and recategorizing them based on how important they are in creating the output. As a result, these findings can then be used to segregate images that look similar to one another. Because of this, pixel differences can be noted, which may not be visible to the human eye.

4) The Deconvolutional Neural Network:
These are also known as "DNNs". As their name suggests, they work in the opposite fashion to how a CNN would. They first start with processing the initial datasets that they have been fed, and literally work backwards until a comprehensible image (which is the output) can be created. DNNs are typically

used to locate and identify information discarded by or missed when using a CNN.

5) The Modular Neural Network:

These are also known as "MNNs". This can be viewed as a hybrid approach, since multiple Neural Networks are used together to create a process known as "Ensemble Learning". This is where the different Neural Networks come together to pool results and come to a consensus towards the common goal: Computing the desired output.

6) The Transformer:

This is a newer and much more advanced type of Neural Network in which "self-attention layers" are used. Put in simpler terms, as it relates to ChatGPT, this kind of particular model will closely examine a sentence, whether it is spoken or written, in order to determine its context.

The Theoretical Constructs of Artificial Neural Networks

There are six major theoretical considerations of an ANN, which are as follows:

1) The activity of a neuron in an ANN is deemed to be an "all or nothing" approach. This simply means the model completely predicts the results of the output, or it is discarded in its entirety.

2) If any of the neurons in the ANN have a statistical weighting of greater than 1, it must then be "excited" within a certain time period.

3) The only acceptable delays in an ANN system are those which are synaptic based.

4) If any neuron is deemed to be "inhibitory" in nature the only preventative action is that the actions of the neurons be halted at a time in the ANN system.

5) The neuron connections that are found in the ANN do not, and should not, change for any reason whatsoever.

6) The neuron in the ANN system is actually composed of a binary format.

The Hebbian Law

Another important aspect of the ANN is what is known as the "Hebbian Law". It can be stated as follows:

> When an Axon of Cell A is near enough to excite the levels of Cell B, and when Cell A takes an active participation in the transmitting of Cell B, then some growth process or metabolic change then takes place in which Cell A is increased which increases its particular efficiency level.[7]

Put in another way, there is a one to one (1:1) mathematical relationship between Cell A (in Neuron A) and Cell B (in Neuron B). If Cell B becomes active, then a direct and positive impact will occur upon the productivity of Cell A. This will optimize the overall process of the ANN in order to derive the desired outputs.

The Associative Memory Principle

This theoretical component states that if a mathematical vector exists in the neuron of an ANN, then that can also be considered to be an input. These statistical weights that have been assigned will have to be further adjusted, so that they can more closely be associated with the datasets that have been ingested into the ANN.

The Winner-Take-All Principle

This theory states that if there are certain neurons that are all receiving the same kind of mathematical vectors, then only one neuron needs to be fired within the ANN system. This particular neuron will then be classified as the one whose statistical input weights will best fit into the ANN system. This all comes down to a standpoint of efficiency. For example, if it just takes one neuron to compute the output, then there is no need to have multiple neurons to carry out the work. The bottom line here is that this will require less processing and computational power on the part of the ANN system.

The Adaline

This is also known as the "Adaptive Linear Neuron" and only refers to one neuron, and not a series of them, in the ANN system. It can be used to build the "bipolar perceptron". Mathematically, it can be represented as follows:

$$Z = W_o + n \sum t = 1\ W_i X_i$$

where W_o is a statistically biased term for the training functionality of the ANN system.

When the Adaline is actually applied to an ANN system, the desired output can be computed as follows:

$$Z = \sum I\, W_i X_i$$

The Madaline

This is also known as the "Many Adaline" and refers to the fact that there are many neurons that are present in the ANN system, not just one. The actual structure of the Madaline is different from that of the Adaline in the sense that only complete outputs can be yielded by the ANN system. Since most ANN systems have multiple neurons in them, it is important to note that they are driven by a specialized statistical technique known as the "Minimum Disturbance Principle", or the "MDP" for short.

The Backpropagation Algorithm

This kind of algorithm is used to assign and implement intermediate statistical weights for the inputs that are used by the ANN system, in order to train the hidden layers that reside within it.

Modified Backpropagation (BP) Algorithms

This is actually a modification of the backpropagation algorithm. It is designed to introduce a certain amount of risk into the ANN system, so that it remains resilient and optimized over a period of time. In order to accomplish this goal, a certain amount of statistical bias or variance has to be introduced. This is done with the following equation:

$$B_i = W_{oi}{}^* B$$

where W_{oi} is the statistical weight that is assigned to the input of the associated neuron. As noted previously, this level of variance can hold either a positive or a negative mathematical value.

The Hopfield Network

This type of ANN algorithm also has multiple layers attached to it. With this kind of approach, any "feedback" solicited from the neurons that are used can also compute the values of the outputs.

The Counterpropagation Network

The principles for this lie in what is known as "Kohonen Self-Organizing Mapping", or "SOM". It also makes use of Unsupervised Learning, which was reviewed earlier in this chapter. The primary disadvantage of this is that it cannot be used for a wide range of applications, because it requires an enormous amount of both processing and computing power.

The LAMSTAR

This is an acronym that stands for the "LArge Memory STorage and Retrieval" network. There are three key advantages of using this theoretical concept, and they are as follows:

1) Kantian Based Link Weights Are Used:
   These are used to connect the multiple layers of the neuron. This then allows the ANN system to integrate other inputs of various types and dimensions, such as images.
2) The Feature Map:
   This is a graphical feature that displays the activity of the neurons firing within the ANN system.
3) Graduated Forgetting:
   This allows the ANN system to continue in a seamless fashion and still compute the correct output even if there are large chunks of datasets that are missing during the ingestion period.

Two LAMSTAR networks, known as the "LAMSTAR-1" and the "LAMSTAR-2", should be noted. These kinds of Neural Networks are specifically designed for applications when it comes to retrieval, analysis, classification, prediction, and decision making. They are also meant to be used with Big Data datasets. Also, the LAMSTAR networks can handle both quantitative and qualitative data. Further, they can also be used to help estimate any kind or type of missing data in the datasets via the technique of "extrapolation". Finally, the LAMSTAR has proven to be very successful with those applications that typically deal with decision making and recognition.

The Adaptive Resonance Theory
This is known as "ART" for short. The goal of this AI theory is to create, develop, and deploy an ANN system with regards to recognizing patterns and classifying them. This is technically known as "plasticity". Simply put, the ANN system becomes a central repository of everything that it has learned and will continue to learn in the future.

The ART consists of three layers, which are as follows:

1) The Comparison Layer:
   A binary element is entered into the neuron of the comparison layer.
2) The Recognition Layer:
   This is a variant of the "classification layer". The various inputs that it receives are mathematically derived from the "n" dimensional weight vector "d". This is based on the property known as the "lateral inhibition connection". This is where the output of each neuron (denoted by "I") is connected via an "inhibitory" connection weighted matrix.
3) The Gain and Reset Elements:
   These are elements which produce scalar outputs to all of the neurons in the ANN system. A scalar output can be technically defined as follows:

   A scalar-output function is a numerical-output function whose function range is a real number interval.[8]

The Cognitron
The cognitron is a specialized type of ANN that has been designed for the deployment of Pattern Recognition. In order to do this, the cognitron based Neural Network makes total use of both the inhibitory and excitatory neurons. This kind of ANN is also considered to be a "Deep Learning" type of model.

An inhibitory neuron can be technically defined as follows:

> Inhibitory neurons usually tell other neurons *not* to fire. They are less plentiful than excitatory neurons but more diverse. In some ways, they are the real brains of the system, the machines in the background that pace and coordinate a ceaseless hum of electrical activity.[9]

In other words, the human brain has a system of "checks and balances in place". These kinds of neurons keep the brain in check but keep the stimulation to an acceptable level.

An excitatory neuron can be technically defined as follows:

> [They] have excitatory effects on the neuron. This means they increase the likelihood that the neuron will fire an action potential.[10]

In other words, these are the kinds of neurons that will stimulate activity with other neurons, in order to catalyze the processes within the human brain.

It is important to note at this point that there are eight main types of excitatory neurons, which are as follows:

1) Acetylcholine:
   This is found throughout the nervous system of the human body. Its main function is muscle stimulation, including those of the gastrointestinal system.
2) Epinephrine:
   This is also known commonly as "adrenaline", and is produced by the adrenal glands. It increases the heart rate, blood pressure, and glucose production.
3) Glutamate:
   This balances the effects of gamma-aminobutyric acid (GABA), an inhibitory neurotransmitter.
4) Histamine:
   This regulates the immune system against foreign entities like allergens.
5) Dopamine:
   This is linked to reward mechanisms in the human brain.

6) Norepinephrine:
   This is found in the sympathetic nervous system, and regulates vital functions such as heart rate, blood pressure, etc.
7) Gamma-Aminobutyric Acid:
   This is also known as "GABA". It has a large presence in the human brain and reduces neuronal excitability in the entire nervous system.
8) Serotonin:
   This regulates emotion and mood, the sleep cycle, carbohydrate cravings, food digestion, and pain management.

The Neocognitron
With this, there are two groups of layers, which are composed of both simple cells and multi-layered cells. There is also a three-tiered layer approach. This has been specifically designed so that the neocognitron can overpower the various recognition issues that were not resolved by the cognitron. Examples of this include images that are in the wrong kind of position or have any sort of angular distortions.

Recurrent Backpropagation Networks
As their name suggests, the outputs from the ANN system can be automatically fed back into the ANN system as inputs. But this can only be achieved in small amounts at a time. There is also a minimal number of hidden layers. Delay mechanisms are also embedded into the ANN system so that the various feedback loops will be totally independent of each other, known technically as "epochs". Also, any statistical errors that are associated with the outputs can be shunted back as inputs for the next iteration in the ANN system. For example, if an ANN system receives the inputs as "X1" and "X2", this will count as a first time iteration, thus fully eliminating any kinds of previous statistical errors.

Fully Recurrent Networks
In this kind of ANN, the outputs are looped back in as layers, not as inputs. So, at the end of any iteration, the output layer will be fed back as the input layer.

Continuously Recurrent Backpropagation Networks
Each iteration in the ANN system goes on forever, but over time they become shorter in both time and nature.

Deep Neural Networks
These are also known as "DNNs" They are specialized types of ANNs in which a certain level of "Deep Learning" is reached. They can be technically defined as follows:

> Deep learning is a subset of machine learning that uses multi-layered neural networks, called deep neural networks, to simulate the complex decision-making power of the human brain.[11]

Deep Learning can probe into very complex datasets that are both qualitative and quantitative in nature (also known as "Big Data"). It can locate hard to find hidden trends in the datasets that are ingested into a DNN. DNNs also make use of very sophisticated statistical techniques, which include the following:

- Heuristic methods.
- Deterministic techniques.
- Stochastic techniques.

A key facet of Deep Learning is what is known as "integration". This is where Big Data datasets must all work together so that the ANN can literally "digest" them. As with any AI system, one of the key goals of Deep Learning is to ensure that the outputs that are generated will not be skewed or biased in any way, shape, or form.
At the present time, there are two different versions of Deep Learning, which are as follows:

1) Deep Boltzmann Machines (DBMs):
   These are considered to be stochastic based kinds of Neural Networks. For data ingestion to happen, "thermodynamic equilibrium" is utilized, which is based upon the Gibbs–Boltzmann statistical distribution. The learning process is done through a special technique called "log-likelihood", where the statistical errors between the datasets and the ANN system model are scrutinized.

2) Deep Recurrent Learning Neural Networks (DRNs):
This kind of Deep Neural Network makes specific use of the backpropagation technique. The layers arc stacked in a linear pattern at different time gaps. This kind of ANN system is typically used in modeling various programming languages.

Finally, in this chapter, we have reviewed:

- Artificial Intelligence.
- Machine Learning.
- Neural Networks.

Notes

1 www.ibm.com/topics/rpa
2 www.sas.com/en_us/insights/analytics/what-is-artificial-intelligence.html
3 Tauli, Tom. (2019). *Artificial Intelligence Basics: A Non-Technical Introduction.* Apress.
4 https://mitsloan.mit.edu/ideas-made-to-matter/machine-learning-explained
5 https://towardsdatascience.com/what-the-hell-is-perceptron-62621 7814f53
6 www.askhandle.com/blog/neurons-and-weights-in-neural-networks
7 Tauli, 2019.
8 www.gabormelli.com/RKB/Scalar-Output_Function#:~:text=A%20sca lar%2Doutput%20function%20is,range%3A%20Real%20Numbers
9 www.the-scientist.com/opinion-the-overlooked-power-of-inhibitory-neurons-68819#:~:text=Inhibitory%20neurons%20usually%20tell%20ot her,PEGASUS%20BOOKS%2C%20JUNE%202021
10 www.healthline.com/health/excitatory-neurotransmitters#what-neurot ransmitters-do
11 www.ibm.com/topics/deep-learning

3

INTRODUCTION TO GENERATIVE AI, NATURAL LANGUAGE PROCESSING, AND THE DIGITAL PERSON

Introduction

So far in this book, we have reviewed in detail what phishing is all about and how horrible threat variants have emerged from it, as of today. The one particular variant that has really become nasty is that of ransomware. We provided a definition of what it is exactly and what the ramifications are if a ransom payment is actually made. We also examined ways in which ransomware could be mitigated, especially from the standpoint of creating adequate backups.

Preference was given to using a backup system in the Cloud, on the basis of the many advantages that it has to offer. Another threat variant that has at least indirectly stemmed from phishing is that of the Dark Web. For example, after data has been exfiltrated from a phishing attack, it is often sold here. One way to mitigate this risk from happening is by conducting what is known as a "Dark Web Scan", which was also reviewed in detail.

This then brings up the next major variant that has occurred from phishing. And that is, the extortion attack. For example, rather than simply selling the stolen data on the Dark Web, the cyberattacker could very well threaten the victim by exposing this data to the public if a higher ransom payment is not made. The different types of extortion attacks were examined. Towards the end of the chapter, we took a closer look at what Artificial Intelligence (AI) is all about at a high level, and

   DOI: 10.1201/9781003503781-3

also, we looked at the major components that constitute a complete AI system, with a special emphasis on the importance of datasets.

After providing this overview of AI, we then examined how it can be used to launch various kinds of phishing attacks. From here, a segue was then made into what Generative AI is on a high level, and some of the other major components that are associated with it, especially that of Prompt Engineering. Finally, an overview was then provided of the major security risks that are posed by Generative AI, and how they can be "spilled over" into creating newer, stealthier, and much more deceptive phishing attacks.

In Chapter 2, we did a much more technical deep dive into AI. For example, we examined its overall evolutionary history. We then segued into Machine Learning, which is deemed even today to be a crucial aspect of AI. In this, a review was provided of the two training techniques of Machine Leaning and how the entire Machine Learning process takes place. We also looked at some of the major Machine Learning algorithms, and even looked at a very high level as to what the perceptron is all about.

The rest of Chapter 2 examined the Neural Network extensively, as this is also a very critical aspect of AI. A definition of it was provided, and an extensive review of the neuron was given. The primary reason for this is that it too is a very critical component whenever an AI model is built.

A formal definition of a Neural Network was provided, and from there, an introduction to the Artificial Neural Network (also known as the "ANN"). The overall model of the ANN was examined, and the various, specific ANN models that can be created were also examined. Finally, an extensive review of the theoretical constructs surrounding the ANN was also provided, as well as the major theorems that are associated with it.

With this very solid background that was provided on phishing and AI, we now look more closely at a new and emerging field of AI – that of Generative AI.

An Introduction to Generative AI

As has been described throughout this book so far, AI is really nothing new. It has evolved since the 1940s, and has made continual, steady progress since then. But what is different about AI now is that it is easily accessible to anybody who wants to use it, something that never occurred before. The primary catalyst for this happening is the dawn of Generative AI. Although we provided a definition of it earlier in this book, it is important to review another, technical definition of it. So, here it is:

> Generative AI enables users to quickly generate new content based on a variety of inputs. Inputs and outputs to these models can include text, images, sounds, animation, 3D models, or other types of data.[1]

So as one can see, there are a number of key differences between Generative AI and the traditional AI that was reviewed in the last chapter. Here are some of them:

- As was described earlier, traditional AI is merely viewed as "Garbage In, Garbage Out". This simply means that the output produced is 100% dependent upon the inputs that are fed, which are the datasets. In contrast, Generative AI can look beyond the datasets that it has been trained upon. For example, it can find on its own other resources on the Internet through the superior Unsupervised Learning that it has achieved.
- Generative AI can produce many other kinds of outputs, as has been explained in the definition earlier. For example, it can provide the outputs as images, video, or even as audio. Or if the end user prefers, they can even get the traditional text based format as well.
- Unlike traditional AI, Generative AI can create fresher levels of content for its output. This simply means that the output will be far more robust, given its ability to search for different resources in response to the query.
- With traditional AI, you are rather limited in how your query can be structured. As a result, this will greatly limit the quality of the output that you will receive. But with Generative AI, there is much more freedom and flexibility to create the query that will get the output you are looking for. As was reviewed in

Chapter 2, this is also technically "Prompt Engineering". But the drawback here is that you have to have some higher level of expertise in order to create the "perfect query". This can take a great deal of time to accomplish, as it can only be learned via trial and error.

- Traditional AI is best suited to heavy data analysis and finding hidden trends in large datasets (also known as "Big Data"), and it is pretty much limited to just that, although this functionality can serve a wide variety of industries, such as healthcare and insurance. In contrast, Generative AI has a wider range of applications that it can be used in, and thus it can serve more markets and industries in this regard.

The Latest Example of Generative AI

At this point in time, one of the best examples of Generative AI is that of ChatGPT. This is reviewed in more detail in the next two subsections:

The Origins of ChatGPT

This platform was originally developed by OpenAI. It first came out in November 2022, so it is still a fairly new application. Technically, ChatGPT is built upon OpenAI's GPT-3.5 and GPT-4 algorithms of what are known as "Large Language Models", or "LLMs". Further, these specific algorithms were optimized using both Supervised and Unsupervised AI Learning techniques. However, as of March 2023, ChatGPT is now powered by the GPT-4 algorithm, which is the latest release from OpenAI.

The Technicalities and Specifications Behind ChatGPT

ChatGPT comes from the family of generative pre-trained transformer language models (this is where the "GPT" part of the name comes from). As just mentioned, it uses both Supervised and Unsupervised Learning. It should be noted that human intervention was needed to help optimize the performance of ChatGPT. In terms of Supervised

Learning, the model was given real life conversations in which the developers played both sides of the fence: the end user as well as the Virtual Assistant.

With Unsupervised Learning, the developers created ranked responses that the model had formulated based upon previous conversations. From here, these quantitative based rankings were then used for the development of the "reward models". These were eventually used to further optimize the model by making use of Proximal Policy Optimization algorithms, also known as the "PPO".

At the present time, OpenAI collects information and data from the many ChatGPT end users as feedback. This is then used to train and optimize the back-end algorithms even more. With this mechanism, the end user can either "upvote" (positive) or "downvote" (negative) the responses they receive from ChatGPT and how useful they were for them in the project that they were trying to accomplish.

The Disadvantages of ChatGPT

Of course, the advantages of ChatGPT are enormous; as mentioned, it can serve a huge amount of applications. Throughout this book thus far, we have elaborated on the key features of AI, Machine Learning, and Neural Networks. But it is very important to keep in mind that there are disadvantages as well, which need to reviewed. The following are some that are associated with ChatGPT, but they can also be extrapolated to other areas of Generative AI as well. Here are some of them:

* The output may not be what the end user is expecting, which is technically known as "hallucination".
* It can become overtrained and not give the correct or expected output. This phenomenon is also known as "optimization pathology".
* It is prone to "algorithmic bias". This is where one output is highly favored over the alternatives.
* Although the outputs are wide, it can only accept inputs from the end user in text format.
* It is unable to multitask. This simply means that you can only present one query at a time to it.

* Because of the level of sophistication of its algorithms, it takes a lot of overhead in terms of both computing and processing power.
* AI algorithms can go "stale" quickly over a short period of time. Therefore, there is the constant need to keep them updated, refined, and optimized at all times.
* Not enough detail may be provided, especially for complex queries.

The Different Kinds of Generative AI Models

In the world of Generative AI, there are three kinds of models that exist. Just like Artificial Neural Networks (ANNs, as reviewed in Chapter 2), they can also, to some degree, be customized to fit your business or scientific requirements. The four models that are widely used today are as follows:

1) The Diffusion Models:
   These are also referred to as "Denoising Diffusion Probabilistic Models", or "DDPMs" for short. Using a two-step methodology, they can easily determine the mathematical vectors mapped onto a Cartesian geometric plane. This methodology is broken down as:
   • Forward Diffusion:
     This process adds random variance and/or bias to the training data datasets that are fed into the Generative AI model.
   • Reverse Diffusion:
     In this process, the datasets can actually be recreated from the bias and/or noise first introduced in the forward diffusion process.
   Traditionally, diffusion models can take a very long time to train, but by using the aforementioned two-step process, the speed of training has been greatly increased. It should also be noted at this point that diffusion models are also grouped as "foundation models".
2) The Variational Autoencoders:
   These are also known as "VAEs". They contain two kinds of Neural Networks, which are the encoder and the decoder.

When given a particular dataset, the encoder converts it into a random representation of it. The decoder then reconstructs this dataset, in an effort to eradicate any kind or type of statistical noise (also known as "outliers"). The encoder and decoder work together to learn an efficient and simple latent data representation. This allows the end user to experiment with different kinds of datasets in an efficient manner.

3) The Generative Adversarial Networks:

These are also known more commonly as "GANs". They were actually developed back in 2014 and have formed one of the foundations for Generative AI. Also, here there are two Neural Networks that are being used, which are as follows:

- The Generator:
  This creates new representations of the datasets that were ingested into it.
- The Discriminator:
  This determines if the representations that were produced in the generator are real or fake.

  The primary objective of this counter-process is to create an output that is almost indistinguishable from a real-world object.

4) The Transformer Network:

This is very similar to the Recurrent Neural Network, as reviewed in Chapter 2. With this kind of Generative AI model, the goal is to process the datasets in a manner that is not deemed to be linear. Thus, qualitative based datasets, such as video, images, audio, etc., can be processed quickly, with a reduction in both computing and processing power. There are two components to this, which are as follows:

- The Self-Attention Layer:
  This assigns a statistical weight to the datasets that are ingested. This value can vary, because it represents the level of importance of it.
- The Positional Encoding:
  If a contextual output is generated (such as context or text), this will determine the word order so that it will have a logical flow.

The Evaluation of a Generative AI Model

Once you have created your Generative AI model for whatever the purpose might be, it is first very important to evaluate it, or test it in a sandbox like environment before you deploy it in the production environment. Of course, the exact way and criteria will be solely dependent upon your requirements. The following are three key, general criteria that you need to pay very special attention to:

1) The Quality:
   As has been the theme throughout this book so far, the prime determinant in the quality and robustness of your outputs is directly a function of the datasets and other kinds of inputs that are fed into the Generative AI model. For example, if you want a very high quality image as the output, then you will need to input the same level of quality in the beginning. Of course, there are also filters that you use to further refine the quality of the images that are used as inputs.

2) The Diversity:
   Equally important as quality is the diversity of the datasets. For example, you do not want to keep feeding the Generative AI model the same kinds of datasets on a real-time basis. If you do this on a consistent basis, both the model and its associated algorithms will go stale and stop producing the required output. Therefore, the datasets that you ingest into the system have to be diverse as well. This will also help keep the Generative AI model trained to look for other resources than what it has been trained on.

3) The Speed:
   The good news here is that since Generative AI is making use of the latest algorithms, the speed at which the output can be calculated is greatly enhanced when compared to using a traditional AI based model. But of course, to keep the high levels of speed up, the datasets have to be cleansed and optimized on a real-time basis as well.

These are illustrated in the diagram here (Figure 3.1) along with the Generative AI model where these aforementioned qualities are needed the most.

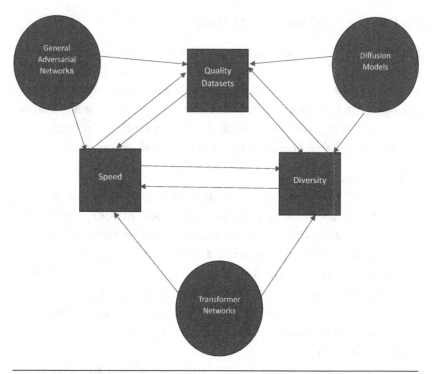

Figure 3.1 These are the key variables that should be used when evaluating the robustness of a Generative AI model.

Generative AI and Large Language Models

There is often a lot of confusion between Large Language Models (also known as "LLMs") and Generative AI. While the latter is used to power the former (especially when it comes to the creation of the "Digital Person"), there are differences between them as well. A technical definition of an LLM is as follows:

> A large language model (LLM) is a type of artificial intelligence (AI) algorithm that uses deep learning techniques and massively large data sets to understand, summarize, generate and predict new content.[2]

In a more focused sense, the goal of an LLM is to try to understand human language, both written and spoken, and try to emulate those processes in having a real life conversation with an end user.

In this regard, there are four kinds of LLM, which are as follows:

1) The Zero Shot Model:
   This is meant for just general use cases, and only general datasets
   are used for them. It is typically the GPT-3 algorithms that
   are used to power this kind of model.
2) The Domain Specific Model:
   This is a type of LLM which serves only one purpose and is
   discarded after its use is over.
3) The Large Representation Model:
   This kind of model makes use of the "Bidirectional Encoder
   Representations from Transformers" (also known as "BERT")
   that are used to drive Natural Language Processing (also known
   as "NLP") models. This is a topic that will be covered later in
   this chapter and in which Generative AI plays a large part.
4) The Multimodal Model:
   This kind of model can produce sophisticated text and image
   outputs. It is the GPT-4 algorithms that power these.

To view an LLM in simpler terms, it can take petabytes of data (and
possibly even more) to try to emulate human language, whether the
inputs are text, audio, image, chat, video, etc. But what makes an LLM
unique is that it attempts to look for the meaning of and correlation
between individual words and phrases that are both spoken and
written. Because of the sheer volume of datasets that they can ingest,
LLMs can understand to some degree how humans speak with one
another, whether in a remote or face to face setting.

This matrix describes the four major LLM algorithms:

ALGORITHM	FEATURES/CHARACTERISTICS
GPT-4	This was developed exclusively by OpenAI and is far more powerful than its predecessor, the GPT-3 algorithms, which laid the foundation for ChatGPT. For any use case, it can generate up to 25,000 words. It has been estimated that there are some 1.76 trillion parameters that make up the GPT-4 algorithm.

(continued)

ALGORITHM	FEATURES/CHARACTERISTICS
The Generalist Language Model (also known as "GLaM")	This is a set of LLM algorithms that was developed by Google. It has some 1.2 trillion parameters that are attached to it. This kind of algorithm is used to create human like responses to any query that is posed to it.
The Bidirectional Encoder Representations from Transformers (also known as "BERT")	Also developed by Google, it is not nearly as powerful as GLaM is. It is only associated with 340 million parameters and is used primarily for answering simple queries, whether in text or in speech.
The Large Language Model Meta AI (also known as "LLaMA")	This algorithm was developed by Meta. It is rumored to have "billions of parameters" attached to it. It is trained in 20 different foreign languages and thus is heavily used for foreign language translation works.

Generative AI and Predictive AI

There is also some confusion between Generative AI and Predictive AI. While the two are used to predict an outcome, the approaches are different.

There are three kinds of Predictive AI models, which are as follows:

1) The Regression Model:

   This is a sophisticated statistical technique used to estimate relationships between a predetermined number of variables. It is primarily to ascertain both known and hidden patterns in large datasets. This kind of AI model is used to determine how one or more independent variables will affect one another.

2) The Decision Tree:

   These are Classification Models that put data into different categories This kind of AI model resembles a tree, with each branch representing a decision to be made. From there, the leaf of a branch represents the result of that decision.

3) The Neural Network:

   This was examined in great detail in Chapter 2. Essentially, these are best utilized to ascertain nonlinear relationships in the datasets.

So as you can see, the sole intention of a Predictive AI model is to make a certain prediction, based upon the datasets that have been ingested into it. To do this, historical time series data is used. The basic hypothesis here is that past trends will accurately predict future trends. Because of this, a great deal of Supervised Learning is required, to make sure that the datasets are updated on a daily basis.

The primary disadvantage of Predictive AI is that the output is only as good as its training datasets. This is the key difference here when compared to Generative AI.

A Review of Generative AI Learning Theories

Back in Chapter 2, we reviewed some of the key learning theories that are used in Machine Learning. These can also be applied not only to Artificial Neural Networks (ANNs), but also to Generative AI. In this subsection, we examine two of them in more detail, which are:

- Unsupervised Learning.
- Semi-Supervised Learning.

1) Unsupervised Learning:
   As described in the last chapter, this is where minimal human intervention is needed to train the Generative AI not only to train on, but to produce the desired outputs. Under the category of Unsupervised Learning, there are four techniques to do this:
   - Clustering:
     This is when similar looking images are grouped together into one category. For example, if the model sees an Airbus A340 and a Boeing 747-400, it will discover that they both have four engines attached to them. Thus, the Generative AI model will then group this under the classification of "Jumbo Jets".
   - Anomaly Detection:
     Once again, the prime example of this is that of cybersecurity. To start off with, an IT security team will come up with what is known as a "baseline profile". This indicates what normal behavior looks like. Anything outside of this regime

will fall under suspicious behavior. For example, the baseline profile could state that three attempted logons to a shared server is normal, until a lockout occurs. But if the end user attempts to log in more times after the lockout, then this is deemed to be suspicious behavior.

- Association:
  This is where the Generative AI model will correlate certain features of an object, and from there attempt to extrapolate other characteristics that the object should have. For example, if it sees that 747-400 with four engines, it will surmise that it is used for long distance flying. Therefore, the system will then attempt to come up with other characteristics that validate this hypothesis, such as a longer wing span, longer fuselage, etc.

- Autoencoders:
  This is where the Generative AI model will take a piece of the dataset, convert it into a mathematical code, and from there try to rebuild that image again. With the example of the 747-400, if the Generative AI model examines the Krueger flaps, it will then convert them into a series of mathematical codes. Then from there, it will attempt to recreate the initial image as accurately as possible.

2) Semi-Supervised Learning

With this approach, the Generative AI model makes use of both Supervised Learning and Unsupervised Learning. This is also known technically as the "hybrid approach". Under this particular category, there are two techniques to do this:

- The Generator:
  This technique attempts to create an entirely new dataset based upon those datasets that it has trained on and previously ingested. For example, once the Generative AI model computes the image of a 747-400, it will then try to create a new image of it taking off, in flight, landing, etc.

- The Autogenerator:
  Once the Generative AI model has created the new images from the generator, this technique will then determine if

these new images should be used as datasets that should be ingested back into the Generative AI model.

A Formal Generative AI Project Plan

Before you even start building a Generative AI model, it is first imperative that you come up with a Project Plan. At a high level, you should map out what your objectives are and what the desired outputs will be. Then you need to consider probably the most important factors: the datasets that you plan to ingest into the Generative AI model, and how they will be cleansed and optimized. The following matrix details the steps that you need to take in order to complete this Project Plan:

PHASE	WHAT NEEDS TO BE ACCOMPLISHED
Phase 1: Identify the Goals	The overall objectives of what you want your Generative AI model to accomplish, all of the key challenges that will be faced, and how they will be resolved.
Phase 2: Data Identification and Preparation	The datasets have to identified, in terms of what their sources will be, as well as the procedures for how they will be "cleansed" and optimized before ingestion into the Generative AI model.
Phase 3: Pick the Right Algorithm	The appropriate algorithms need to be carefully studied and picked, and further enhanced to meet the specific objectives.
Phase 4: Create the Model Architecture	This is where the individual components of the Generative AI model will come together and be assembled. This includes the neurons, connections, layers, etc.
Phase 5: Training, Validation, and Testing	This involves three substeps: *Training the Generative AI model (Training). *Confirming that the datasets are cleansed and optimized (Validation). *Confirming the effectiveness of the Generative AI model (Testing).

(continued)

PHASE	WHAT NEEDS TO BE ACCOMPLISHED
Phase 6: Deployment	This is where the Generative AI model is implemented into the production environment and used to predict the outcomes of different scenarios or provide the answers to queries. This is technically known as the "output".
Phase 7: Continuous Evaluation and Optimization	This is where the Generative AI model will be further evaluated over time, and further tweaked and/or enhanced so that it remains robust at all times.

These steps are illustrated in Figure 3.2:

COTS Based Generative AI Platforms

COTS is an acronym that stands for "Commercial Off The Shelf". As it relates to Generative AI, you do not actually have to create your models from scratch. Rather, there are numerous platforms that are available on a commercial basis, which you can start using quickly. Here is a review of some of the major ones:

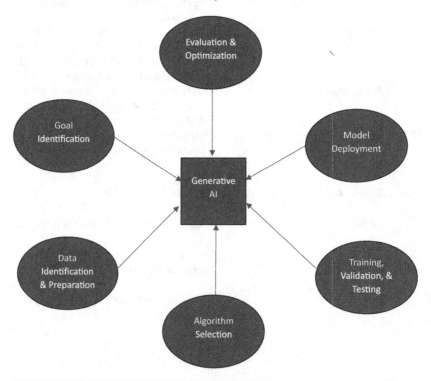

Figure 3.2 These are the steps of an AI project plan.

1) PaLM 2:

This is an acronym that stands for "Pathways Language Model", and it was developed by Google. It is powered by the GPT-3/GPT-4 algorithms and a Transformer Neural Network. Its core functionalities include the following:

- Text Generation.
- Summarization: It can create summaries of lots of content in a shorter form.
- Content Analysis: This allows for the end user to fully understand the sentiment and context of a given block of text.
- Reasoning.
- Source Code Generation: It can create code for web based applications in 80 different languages, including Java, JavaScript and Python. It can also identify any vulnerabilities within the source code.
- Text Translation: It can be extensively used in foreign language translation applications.

More detailed information about PaLM 2 can be found at: https://ai.google/discover/palm2/

2) Bard:

This was reviewed in one of the previous subsections of this chapter. As of February 2024, the name was changed to "Gemini". This too was developed by Google and is totally powered by Large Language Models (LLMs) and the Language Model for Dialogue Applications (also known as LaMDA). Just like ChatGPT, Bard (Gemini) can also be used for creative purposes. Other ways it can be used include the following:

- Image Processing: It can go through complex images such as charts, figures, diagrams, and heavily pixelated images.
- Audio Processing: It can be used for speech/voice recognition applications.
- Video Understanding: It can process video frames to create metadata such as descriptions.

- Different Layers of Reasoning: This is also known as "multimodal reasoning" and is primarily used as an aid for creating Prompt Engineering based queries.

More detailed information about Bard can be found at: http://cyberresources.solutions/GenAI_Book/BARD_Overv iew.pdf

3) The Amazon Titan:

This has been developed by Amazon Web Services (AWS). It serves these key areas:

- Text Generation.
- Content Summary Generation.
- Image Generation.
- Semantic Search: This functionality allows for personalization experiences for end users, especially where Digital Persons are used.
- Retrieval Augmented Generation: This is also known as "RAG". It can be technically defined as follows:

RAG provides a way to optimize the output of an LLM with targeted information without modifying the underlying model itself; that targeted information can be more up-to-date than the LLM as well as specific to a particular organization and industry. That means the generative AI system can provide more contextually appropriate answers to prompts as well as base those answers on extremely current data.[3]

Simply put, the goal is to keep the Generative AI model as up to date as possible, without having to redevelop the entire model again. More information about the AWS Titan can be found at: https://aws.amazon.com/bedrock/ titan/?gclid=EAIaIQobChMI1Lzj39z0hAMVfg-DAx0D CAz1EAAYASAAEgIXWvD_BwE&trk=0eaabb80- ee46-4e73-94ae-368ffb759b62&sc_channel=ps&ef_id= EAIaIQobChMI1Lzj39z0hAMVfg-DAx0DCAz1EAAY ASAAEgIXWvD_BwE:G:s&s_kwcid=AL!4422!3!69200 6004685!e!!g!!amazon%20titan!21048268554!15963 9952775

4) The Azure OpenAI:

At the present time, this is the behemoth of Generative AI usage and deployment. This service was created as a result of the partnership between OpenAI and Microsoft, as reviewed earlier in this chapter. The core algorithms for this are all GPT-4 faced, which is now considered to be the most advanced Generative AI algorithm available today. The best place to get this is on the Microsoft Azure Marketplace, which can be found in your Cloud subscription. Further information about this can be found at:

https://azure.microsoft.com/en-us/products/ai-services/openai-service/?ef_id=_k_EAIaIQobChMIwM6A1eD0hAMVO25HAR1CfAtsEAAYASAAEgJ8pPD_BwE_k_&OCID=AIDcmm5edswduu_SEM__k_EAIaIQobChMIwM6A1eD0hAMVO25HAR1CfAtsEAAYASAAEgJ8pPD_BwE_k_&gad_source=1&gclid=EAIaIQobChMIwM6A1eD0hAMVO25HAR1CfAtsEAAYASAAEgJ8pPD_BwE

The Use Cases and Applications of Generative AI

As Generative AI continues to advance in terms of both technology and growth, the number of use cases and applications is expected to drastically pick up. The following are market sectors where Generative AI has started to make its mark, or potentially will at some subsequent point in time.

1) Increasing Employee Productivity:

Unfortunately, this kind of market application is a double edged sword. On the one hand, the automation that Generative AI can bring can make a business much more efficient, but at the same time, it could mean that the jobs of employees could also be at risk. This is one of the biggest social implications of Generative AI right now, and will continue to be for a long time to come. But in this regard, here is how it can be used:

- Creating specific automation tasks to help employees get their projects and other work related tasks done more quickly.
- In terms of software development, it can be used to help generate new source code (thus alleviating the need to rely exclusively on open source APIs which can be a huge security risk).
- Creating reports on an automated basis. This is particularly useful for the supply chain and logistics industries.

2) The Insurance Industry:

This is one market segment where there is a much higher risk of fraud taking place. Thus, Generative AI can be used here to compare any filed claims against the baseline profiles to see if anything is out of the ordinary. Other use cases include the following:

- Assisting in the underwriting process.
- Processing of submitted claims.
- Creating any quotes and content for insurance policies, as requirements and circumstances change.
- Offering greater levels of customer service by using the Digital Person to interact face to face with the customer. The obvious benefit here is that this will alleviate the current wait times, and customers will get a much quicker response to their queries.

3) The Financial Industry:

The use of Neural Networks has been predominant here, in fact for quite some time. They have been designed and tested to see how accurate an AI model is in predicting future prices of both stocks and commodities, in an effort to make profitable trades. Other applications include the following:

- Generate "what if" scenarios to help rebalance the financial portfolios of clients.
- Conduct risk simulations for the client, in order to reduce the shock of drastic market fluctuations.

- Create model portfolios for financial advisers.
- Assist in the loan underwriting and mortgage approval processes.

4) The Healthcare Industry:

It is expected that this market segment will see one of the greatest uses of Generative AI. It can serve a lot of purposes, all the way from conducting telehealth appointments to data processing to helping medical professionals find new solutions to health ailments, such as cardiac disease and cancer. Other use cases include the following:

- The conversion of X-rays and CT scans into more decipherable and realistic images.
- Using General Adversarial Networks ("GANs") to create detailed sketches of actual surgical procedures to explain surgical plans to patients.
- The possible identification of diseases from submitted pathology images.

In fact, Gartner makes the following predictions as to the market potential of Generative AI:

- "We believe that by 2025, more than 30% of new drugs and materials will be systematically discovered using generative AI techniques, up from zero today. Generative AI looks promising for the pharmaceutical industry, given the opportunity to reduce costs and time in drug discovery".
- We predict that by 2025, 30% of outbound marketing messages from large organizations will be synthetically generated, up from less than 2% in 2022. Text generators like GPT-3 can already be used to create marketing copy and personalized advertising.[4]

The Advantages and Disadvantages of Generative AI

As with any other technology, Generative AI has both its benefits and shortcomings. We now review these in the next two subsections.

The Advantages of Generative AI

1) Creativity Is Enhanced:

   Given the power of the recent GPT-4 algorithms, any new images, audio, video, or even content can be created literally "on the fly". This becomes especially advantageous for last minute sales meetings with prospects and/or customers.

2) Cost and Time Savings:

   Depending upon both the industry and market applications that Generative AI is being used in, it can be a huge advantage when it comes to task automation. Typical examples of these are robotic process automation (also known as "RPA", and reviewed earlier in this book), the creation of engineering drafts and designs, and even in cybersecurity when it comes to both penetration testing and threat hunting.

3) Enhanced Customer Experience:

   One of the best examples of this are call centers. Usually, the agents are totally inundated helping customers to resolve their problems and/or queries. As a result, the wait times can really mount up, thus causing a much heightened level of frustration for the end user. But by using a Digital Person (this will be reviewed later in this chapter), prompt attention can be given very quickly, resulting in greater satisfaction for the customer. This in turn could lead to a sharp increase in repeat business for an organization.

4) Enhanced Levels of Productivity:

   Trying to figure out new work schedules for employees for a certain time period can no doubt be a very laborious and time-consuming task, especially if you are making use of a spreadsheet. But by making use of Generative AI, you can create a brand new work schedule literally within minutes, and even go out as far in time as you need to. In fact, this is where Computer Vision (another branch of AI) can come into play. In this regard, it can be technically defined as follows:

   Computer vision is a field of artificial intelligence (AI) that uses machine learning and neural networks to teach computers and systems to derive meaningful information from digital images, videos and other visual inputs – and to make recommendations or take actions when they see defects or issues.[5]

In this instance, you can present an image of a work schedule spreadsheet to the Generative AI model, and from there it can present an image of a new work schedule for your employees for, say, the next two weeks.

5) Creating Virtual Simulations:

In the past, companies would have to first build a prototype in order to test a product before it could be released into the production environment. This of course meant that a great deal of money, time, and resources would have to be spent in building it. But by using Generative AI here, these kinds of prototypes can be created in a very short time period, making used of a virtualized environment. Because of this, many "what if" scenarios can thus be created, without having to build a brand new prototype each time.

6) Use in Big Data Datasets:

The term "Big Data" has been used frequently throughout this book. A technical definition of it is as follows:

Big data refers to data that is so large, fast or complex that it's difficult or impossible to process using traditional methods. The act of accessing and storing large amounts of information for analytics has been around for a long time.[6]

As you can see, this is a nearly impossible task for a human being to sift through, because it would take so much time to accomplish. But by making use of Generative AI here, these huge datasets can be combed through in a matter of minutes, with the added bonus being that unhidden trends can be seen as well. These can then be used to make future predictions, not only for the business in question but also to stay ahead of the competition.

7) Quicker Times for Drugs:

In the past, it could take a pharmaceutical company years to bring a drug to market. But the COVID-19 pandemic cut this time down drastically, as new vaccinations were created by Pfizer and Moderna in just a matter of months. But by using Generative AI, this time can be brought down even further, especially when it comes to the clinical trials. Google has created an AI tool for this very purpose, and it is called the "Alpha Fold". More information about this can be found at: https://deepmind.google/discover/blog/alphafold-reveals-the-structure-of-the-protein-universe/

8) Improved Decision Making:

Also in this regard, Generative AI can be used to help improve the decision making process for businesses. For example, different queries can be asked of it, and different outputs can then be compared to see the best route. The Digital Person can also be used here as well.

The Disadvantages of Generative AI

For this, the biggest fear is that of cybersecurity.

1) The Launching of Cyberattacks:

Many people are fearful that the cyberattacker of today can easily use Generative AI to create malicious code and deploy it as a threat variant. The following are also some other concerns in this regard:

- The creation of extremely sophisticated deepfakes that even a cyberspecialist will not be able to distinguish from the real thing.
- It can be used to launch social engineering attacks. For example, given the fact that an output of a Generative AI model is an audio file, a very real but fake voice can be used to engage in a conversation with an unsuspecting victim. Eventually, the goal here would be to have them give out their confidential information over a period of time, once a certain level of "fake" trust has been reached.
- Generative AI can also be used to launch massive supply chain attacks, as was exemplified by the SolarWinds security breach.

2) Data Leakages/Data Privacy:

As has been a common theme throughout this book so far, no matter if it is Machine Learning, Neural Networks, or Generative AI, the AI model needs a huge amount of datasets to train on. Also, these datasets must be cleansed and optimized so that there is no statistical skewness generated in the output. But another huge risk is that of data leakage, whether it is intentional or not. This risk is further compounded if these datasets are stored on a Cloud based platform such as that of AWS or Microsoft Azure. The primary reason for this is that the business often relies on the default settings, and they do not customize per their own security requirements. Also, any datasets that are used to train an AI model are now considered to be Personally Identifiable Information (also known as "PII") data. This means that they will now be subject to data privacy laws such as the CCPA, GDPR, HIPAA, etc. If the right controls are not put in place, the organization could become the target of an audit and face steep financial penalties.

3) Skewness in the Output:

As has been stated throughout this book, this is another risk with Generative AI. No matter how optimized and cleansed the datasets might be, and no matter how much it has been trained, there is always the risk that the output may not be accurate. Thus, that is why many AI vendors strongly caution end users to check the results of the output first before submitting it anywhere else. The technical term for this is known as "overfitting" the model.

4) The Explainability Factor:

No matter how many advancements are made in Generative AI, it still suffers from the "black box" phenomenon. This simply means that you feed in the datasets, and the output comes next. There is no way of knowing what happens in between or the process that was used to generate the output. This can be particularly disturbing if somebody used Generative AI to create an answer to a query but cannot provide feedback on how the answer was arrived at.

5) Breaches of Copyright and Intellectual Property (IP):

As has been discussed in this chapter, one of the popular uses of ChatGPT is for creating new content, such as creating a manuscript for a new book. The main problem here is that in order to create this new content, ChatGPT has to rely on other, previous content as the datasets. As a result of this, the new manuscript can contain content that is a direct replication of another previously published work. This is a very serious infringement of both copyright and intellectual property laws. In fact, there have been lawsuits already filed to this effect.

In the next section of this chapter, we look at yet another component of AI that also provides the engine for Generative AI – Natural Language Processing.

An Introduction to Natural Language Processing

A key component of Generative AI is what is known as "Natural Language Processing", or "NLP" for short. This can actually be viewed as yet another subset of Machine Learning as it is crucial when it comes to creating audio outputs or giving a Digital Person the look and feel of an actual human being. Figure 3.3 illustrates what we have covered so far in this book:

The Tasks of Natural Language Processing

By itself, an NLP model can perform the following tasks:

1) Speech/Voice Recognition:
   This is where the human voice is converted into text format. Although the algorithms that handle this are advancing, there are still some obstacles to be overcome, which include the following:
   • How people speak, e.g. slurring words together.
   • Changes in enunciation, such as different accents.
   • The usage of incorrect grammar.

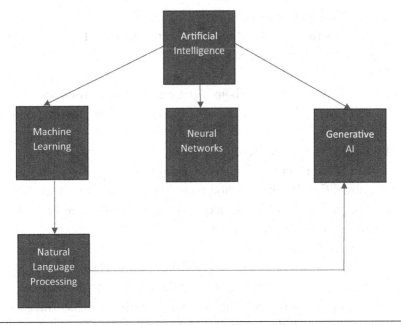

Figure 3.3 This is an overview of all of the AI related models.

2) Part of Speech Tagging:

This is where the NLP model attempts to ascertain which part of speech a word is in a sentence. For example, is it a noun, verb, etc.

3) Word Sense Disambiguation:

This is where semantic analysis is used to segregate the context of a word if it is used in multiple sentences. For example:

- Will I "make" the team? This connotes a sense of "achievement".
- Will I "make" the cake? This connotes a sense of an "action".

4) Named Entity Recognition:

Also technically known as "NEM", this is a part of NLP that tries to identify words and their corresponding phrases with a particular entity. For example, "Boeing 747-400" would be classified as an airplane, and "Indiana" would be classified as a state.

5) Sentiment Analysis:

This is where the NLP model tries to ascertain or gauge the emotional mood of a person.

6) Natural Language Generation:
This is where the NLP model tries to convert a block of text into actual human speech.

7) Tokenization:
This is where the words in a sentence are broken down into different "tokens", which are mathematical representations of them.

8) Natural Language Recognition:
This is often confused with speech to text recognition, but it is quite different. This method takes large blocks of a structured foreign language and breaks them down into more concise, comprehensible blocks of text.

9) Toxicity Classification:
This is a technique used by an NLP model to classify any kind of hostile threat, whether it is spoken or in text. From there, it can put them into different subcategories, such as threats, verbal abuse, bullying, insults, obscenities, etc.

10) Information Retrieval:
This is where an application such as ChatGPT would fit in nicely. For example, once an end user submits a query, the GPT-4 algorithms will try to find the most relevant answer by using either one or even both of the following:
- Indexing:
  This consists of a vector space model, and the subprocess is done using a two tower network model.
- Similarity:
  This is a statistical technique where a system of distance scoring is used to determine the degree of similarity between the resources that are used to compute the output to a query.

11) Lemmatization:
This is a technique where the NLP model breaks a word down into its most basic root form. This is reviewed in more detail in the next subsection.

The Process of Natural Language Processing

The NLP process, given its advanced algorithms, can be accomplished for the most part in just two basic steps, which are as follows:

1) Data Preprocessing:

This is the first step, in which all of the datasets are examined, cleansed, and optimized. Also note that an NLP model can work very well with both quantitative and qualitative based datasets. There are four ways in which this can happen:

- Tokenization:
  This is where sensitive datasets (such as people's private data) are substituted with an irreversible token.
- Stop Word Removal:
  In this instance, all of the common words are removed, so that the most "robust" and meaningful ones remain. This is designed so that the output that is generated will be as realistic as possible.
- Lemmatization/Stemming:
  This is where the words in a qualitative based dataset are broken down into their most basic form. For example, the word "playing" would be reduced to its root form "play". One of the benefits of this is that it will ensure a smoother processing by the NLP model, because of the need for reduced processing and computing resources..
- Part of Speech Tagging:
  This was reviewed in the last subsection, where individual words are categorized based upon how they fit in a sentence, such as a noun, verb, or adjective.

2) Data Processing:

This is the part where the datasets (both quantitative and qualitative based) are processed and used to generate the output. This is where the established algorithms of both Machine Learning and rule based systems have a role. The latter are a series of carefully developed linguistic rules.

In fact, there is a new field of NLP which has started to evolve, and it is called "Natural Language Generation", or "NLG" for short. There are three types of it, which are as follows:

1) Extractive NLG:

This is where a large group of sentences are grouped together, and the most important words and phrases are picked out in order to provide a summary of that particular block of text.

2) Abstractive NLG:

This technique also takes long blocks of text, but rather than summarize them, it tries to create brand new content and language from them.

3) Sequence to Sequence:

This is where the NLP algorithm can take one kind of input and convert it to a different kind of output, while still reaching the overall objective. For example, if an end user wanted to translate a text of English and have that outputted in Arabic, this kind of algorithm would work very well.

Another closely allied area is that of "Natural Language Understanding", also known as "NLU" for short. It can be technically defined as follows:

Natural Language Understanding (NLU) is a field of computer science which analyzes what human language means, rather than simply what individual words say.[7]

Here is an example of how it works:

The query: "tickets New York to Miami 25 April 8pm"
How it is broken down:

"Tickets [intent to buy]
New York [location]
Miami [location]
25 April [date]
8pm [time]"[8]

There are two distinct components to NLP, and these are as follows:

1) Intent Recognition:

This technique tries to ascertain the meaning or the context of the words, as illustrated in the ticket query example.

2) Entity Recognition:

This technique tries to ascertain which words in a sentence or phrase actually refer to a tangible entity. There are two subcategories of this, which are:

- Named Entities:
  These are distinct classifications, such as names of people, businesses, geographic locations, etc.
- Numeric Entities:
  These are numerically based classifications, such as quantities, percentages, currencies, etc.

One of the primary objectives of both NLU and NLG is that the end user wants to feel totally engaged with an AI model; in other words, they want to be heard and responded to like a human being.

It is important to note at this point that NLP also makes heavy usage of both Machine Learning and Deep Learning. The former was reviewed in great detail in the last chapter. But to demonstrate its role in NLP, we illustrate this with a simple example:

In this particular scenario, the output is produced in three distinct steps:

1) The model is trained with an Input/Output (I/O) combination, such as the following:

$$(2 * 10) + (3 * 10) + (5 * 10)$$

This is considered to be the "Preparation and Build" step.

2) The ML algorithms then determine the mathematical relationship as follows:

$$(x * y) + (x * y) + (x * y) = Z$$

This is considered to be the "Training and Tuning" step.

3) We can give this mathematical model an Input/Output of "32", but the actual, computed output will be "100", as denoted by the variable "Z".

This is considered to be the "Deploy and Manage" step and is the last phase.

With regards to Deep Learning, it can be technically defined as follows:

Deep learning models can recognize complex patterns in pictures, text, sounds, and other data to produce accurate insights and predictions. You can use deep learning methods to automate tasks that typically require human intelligence, such as describing images or transcribing a sound file into text.[9]

As its name implies, this takes AI overall into a much more sophisticated analysis, and thus there will be many more layers embedded into it as a result. As it relates to NLP, the following algorithms are the most important:

1) Convolutional Neural Networks:
   These are also referred to as "CovNets". They have four layers that are embedded into them:
   • The Convolutional Layer:
     This filters out for any statistical outliers.
   • The Rectified Layer Unit:
     This is also referred to as the "ReLU". This is the phase where the datasets are actually mapped.
   • The Pooling Layer:
     This is where the dataset is compressed, for the purposes of efficiency.
   • The Fully Connected Layer:
     This is where a mathematical, linear based matrix is created so that any "images" can be recognized in other datasets that have been selected for the initial training of the NLP model.
2) Recurring Neural Networks:
   These are also commonly referred to as "RNNs". This algorithm can learn from previous inputs, thus making it optimal for an NLP model.
3) Long Short-Term Memory Networks:
   These are also commonly referred to as "LSTMNs". They are made up of memory blocks, which store the more relevant information from the datasets. This is how it works:
   • The extraneous data is removed at the "Sigmoid Layer".
   • It is replaced with more pertinent and relevant data.
   • The output is then calculated on the current cell state, based on the last step.

4) General Adversarial Networks:

These are also referred to as "GANs" and have been reviewed earlier in this book. But, for a review, they consist of two distinct parts:

- The Generator:
  This is used to create "fake data", based upon the information that it has been trained on.
- The Discriminator:
  This algorithm checks for the "fake data" and counters it, in an effort to further optimize the NLP model.

5) Multi-Layer Perceptrons:

The concept of the perceptron was introduced in Chapter 2. But in this instance, there are multiple layers of both inputs and outputs, along with various hidden layers. There are also multiple neurons, and they are all interconnected with one another. The datasets are first ingested into the input layer and then subsequently processed to yield the output.

6) Autoencoder:

This is a subset of Deep Learning and is made up of the following components:

- The Encoder:
  This is where the datasets are encoded into a mathematical file format.
- The Code:
  This is where the datasets are broken down into "chunks" for easier ingestion and processing.
- The Decoder:
  This is where the datasets are eventually used for the initial training of the NLP model.

The History of Natural Language Processing

Although Natural Language Processing is now coming to the forefront, it actually does have a very long history, in fact even more so than AI. Here is a timeline of how it has evolved:

1) From 1906–1911:

The first courses in NLP were taught at the University of Geneva, by Professor Saussure. This was also where the concept of an NLP being an actual system was introduced.

2) In 1916:

Albert Sechehaye and Charles Bally took the teachings of Professor Saussure and compiled a book called *Cours de Linguistique Générale*. This manuscript led to the "structuralist approach" that is used in NLP today.

3) In 1950:

Alan Turing composed a scientific paper describing a test for a machine that could "think" on its own. His basic hypothesis was that if a computer could have a primitive conversation with a human being, then it could also "think". This eventually became known as the "Turing Test".

4) In 1952:

The Hodgkin–Huxley model scientifically proved that the human brain creates various "networks" to evoke the thought and reasoning processes. This led to the creation of the first known chatbot, developed by Joseph Weizenbaum. It was called "Eliza", and it was designed to mimic a psychotherapist. But the responses were pre-scripted, and it could not generate answers to queries on its own.

5) In the 1960s:

Scientists created the first version of semantic analysis, parts of speech tagging, and parsing, as well as the first versions of the "corpora", which are machine readable documents that are supplemented with linguistic information and which can subsequently be used to create NLP algorithms.

6) In the 1970s:

The first statistically based algorithms evolved, and the first to come out in this regard was called "SHRDLU". It was developed by Terry Winograd. The first model of this kind was able to produce and move colored blocks in a virtualized environment.

7) In the 1980s:

The first NLP algorithms that relied upon Machine Learning first evolved.

8) In the 1990s:

The development of Deep Learning, Neural Networks, and transformer based models gained increased levels of sophistication. The Hidden Markov Model, also called the "HMM", was developed, and this could convert a spoken phrase into a block of text.

9) In the 2000s:

"Word Embeddings" were created. To this effect, two distinct models were created, which were known as "Word2Vec" and "GloVe". They represented words and blocks of text as "dense vectors". A technical definition of this is as follows:

Dense vectors are a type of mathematical objects that represent data in machine learning and artificial intelligence.[10]

These models could capture the semantics and the relationships between words. For example, the words "computer" and "keyboard" could be represented as mathematical vectors which would display similar geometric patterns.

10) In the 2010s:

Google came out with a new NLP platform which was called the "Neural Machine Translation". This was designed for foreign language translation, while keeping the semantics of the text or spoken language almost identical in the conversion process.

11) In the Present:

ChatGPT is now the de facto Generative AI platform that is being used, powered by transformer models and Large Language Models.

The Tools in Natural Language Processing

Just like in Generative AI, there are also a number of platforms that are available that you can make use of, instead of building your own NLP model from scratch. Here are some of the more widely used tools:

1) Genism:

This tool can recognize the correlations between written and text based language. It also has an indexing function that can handle a large volume of data. More detailed information can be found at:

https://pypi.org/project/gensim/

2) spaCy:

This is deemed to be one of the newer forms of the NLP libraries. It has a plethora of pre-trained models, which can also be used for Deep Learning applications. More information can be found at https://spacy.io/.

3) watsonx:

This is probably one of the best known and most utilized tools in Natural Language Processing. For example, it can determine the keywords that are used in spoken language, and other emotional states that are conveyed by the end user. It is also used quite heavily in both the financial and healthcare sectors. More information about this can be found at www.ibm.com/watson.

4) Natural Language Toolkit:

This is a tool that allows you to create and execute Python based source code to get an overall understanding of human language and the steps that need to be taken to model it. More information can be found at www.nltk.org.

5) MonkeyLearn:

This is powered by NLP algorithms and is used to gain analytical insights from both written and spoken language. One of its key advantages is its powerful sentiment analysis engine. It can also connect to Google and Excel files. More information can be found at https://monkeylearn.com/.

6) TextBlob:

This tool has pre-trained models to perform classification, sentiment analysis, and various kinds of keyword extractions. It also comes with prebuilt Machine Learning models as well. More information can be found at https://textblob.readthed ocs.io/en/dev/.

7) CoreNLP:

This is an NLP model that was developed at Stanford University. It makes use of the Java Development Kit and is used heavily for tokenization and Named Entity Recognition. More details about this platform can be seen at https://stan fordnlp.github.io/CoreNLP/.

8) Google Natural Cloud Language AI:

This is an API that you can use to create source code for NLP based models to do entity extraction, content classification, and sentiment analysis. More information about this platform can be found at https://cloud.google.com/natural-language?hl=en.

The Advantages of Natural Language Processing

Just like Generative AI, Natural Language Processing also has its set of benefits, which are as follows:

1) Big Data:

NLP models can take an enormous amount of data such as images, video, audio, and documents and completely ingest them for training purposes. Further, the NLP model can also make these datasets scalable so that they can be used for any kind of subsequent application.

2) An Objective Analysis:

NLP is quite beneficial in terms of offering an unbiased view of data that you may get from a research instrument such as a survey. Humans can be biased when interpreting the results, and NLP can be a great help here.

3) Improvement in End User Satisfaction:

Another great benefit of an NLP model is that it can run on a 24x7x365 basis. Thus, it would be perfect for the Digital Person (which will be examined in the next subsection), but also for soliciting feedback from end users. In fact, it can also integrate with some of the leading Customer Relation Management (CRM) systems such as Salesforce and Microsoft Dynamics.

4) Foreign Language Automation:

The business world today is expansive; if your business is large enough, there is a good chance that you can have offices in other countries as well as your own. For the employees that work in them, English could very well be a second language. The advantage of NLP here is that your foreign based employees can speak in their native tongue, and this can be translated back into English, by making use of an NLP model. By giving them this kind of flexibility, overall productivity could also be increased as well.

The Disadvantages of Natural Language Processing

Along with the benefits of Natural Language Processing, so come the disadvantages as well. Here is a sampling of them:

1) The Use of Contextual Words:

   Although NLP is getting better at word sense disambiguation, it can still get "confused" if a word is used multiple times in a long block of text. For example:

   "I ran to the store because we ran out of baby formula".

   In this sentence, the word "ran" has two different contextual meanings. An NLP model may not be able to discriminate this, but it can if the sentence is broken down into two, separate sentences:

   "I ran to the store"."I ran out of baby formula".Also, the use of synonyms (in which two different words have the same meaning, such as "shut" and "close") and homonyms (in which two words sound the same, but have a totally different meaning, such as "there" and "their") can also potentially "confuse" an NLP model.

2) The Use of Irony and Sarcasm:

   These are words that are spoken in everyday language and conversations, and as humans, we can do a reasonably good job in discerning them. But this is not the case with an NLP model. For instance, while it can ascertain if a sentence is positive or negative, it cannot determine when the opposite tone to that used is intended. Here is an example:

   "Airline XYX just told me that I will get a refund for my ticket"

   "Yea, right!!!"

   While the NLP model can infer that the first sentence is positive sounding, it will not be able to conclude that the second sentence is negative or sarcastic in nature.

3) Understanding the Different Kinds of Ambiguity:

   Ambiguity refers to sentences or even phrases that can have different interpretations associated with them. There are two specific types of ambiguity, and they are as follows:

- Lexical Ambiguity:
  This is where a word can be used as a verb, noun, or adjective.
- Semantic Ambiguity:
  This is where an entire sentence can be interpreted in two different ways.

4) Errors and Variance in Text and Speech:
This includes the following that the NLP model may not pick up on:

- Misspelled words.
- Misused words.
- Mispronunciations.
- Different accents.
- Stuttering.

5) The Use of Industry Specific Language:
At this point in time, an NLP system cannot be used as a "one size fits all" solution. Meaning, one NLP model cannot be used for different market applications or industries, because each one will have their own lingo and terminology. For example, you would need a dedicated NLP model for each one of them.

6) The Use of Low Resource Languages:
A low resource language can be technically defined as follows:

Low resource languages are those that have relatively less data available for training conversational AI systems.[11]

This refers to less spoken languages (such as Vietnamese, Swahili, Urdu, etc.) for which there is not enough data to feed into an NLP model so that it can learn them. In contrast, the high resource languages (such as English, Chinese, French, Spanish, German, etc.) are far more widely used and spoken, and thus in comparison there is a lot more data here to ingest into an NLP model.

7) Ethical/Social Considerations:
It is important to note that while the primary intention for an NLP model is to make it unbiased, neutral, and objective, they are still inherently not. At this time, they only reflect what has been fed into them, and other, differing resources that they have found in order to compute the output. As a result, they

could greatly magnify the biases and flaws in thinking that exist in the datasets, or even worse, society as a whole.

Finally, one of the best use cases of NLP is that of the Digital Person, which is reviewed in the next section.

An Introduction to the Digital Person

The next evolution from Natural Language Processing and Generative AI is what is known as the "Digital Person". This is how it relates to the other areas of AI as we have reviewed thus far in this book.

The Digital Person can be technically defined as follows:

> Digital people are human-like characters created by combining two primary technologies – computer-generated images and artificial intelligence – to craft a fully autonomous personality. Unlike a chatbot, you can interact with this visible person in lifelike and real conversations.[12]

A Digital Person can also be referred to as one of the following:

- Digital Persona.
- Digital Personality.
- Digital Human.

For the purposes of this book, the term "Digital Person" will be used. As you can see, the Digital Person is essentially the culmination of all of the AI methodologies, with a heavy emphasis upon Generative AI and Natural Language Processing. In fact, the Digital Person will be at the core of our cybersolution to combat phishing; this will be examined in more detail in Chapter 5.

The Replication of a Human Being

Today, a Digital Person can simulate the following, appearing just as an actual human being would:

- Hand and body gestures.
- Facial expressions and other related movements.

- Linguistics, coupled with the fact the Digital Person can also converse in certain foreign languages.
- Appearance to the end user. This includes the following characteristics:

  * The type of clothing (dress up, business casual, formal, etc.).
  * Ethnicity and race.
  * Color of the eyes.
  * Color of the skin.

The primary goal here is to have the Digital Person look appropriate to the industry or market application that it is serving. For example, if the Digital Person were being used in a healthcare setting, it could be designed to be wearing the uniform of a healthcare professional.

The Differences With Earlier Conversational AI Platforms

To this day, there is still some confusion between the Digital Person and its predecessors, namely the chatbot and the Virtual Personal Assistant. Therefore, we take a look at the key differences in these platforms in this section.

The Chatbot

A chatbot can be technically defined as follows:

> A chatbot is a software or computer program that simulates human conversation or "chatter" through text or voice interactions.[13]

Some of the key differentiating features of a chatbot are as follows:

- Quick answers are given only to a specific query.
- The answers are scripted.
- Only preprogrammed options are available, and there is no customization.
- The goal is to take the end user from Point A to Point B in the quickest amount of time possible.

The Virtual Personal Assistant

It should be noted that since VPAs make use of AI, they are considered to be a much more advanced form than the chatbot. For example, as you engage deeper with your VPA, they create a profile about you. From there, they provide suggestions and recommendations as to how you can further enhance the activities that you do on a daily basis.

Another key difference between the chatbot and the VPA is that with the latter, you can ask it far more complex queries. For example, you can ask it to look up which airline flight is available on a certain date and time frame, because the VPA can access the Internet and use other resources to provide an answer. This is something that the chatbot simply cannot do.

Also, the VPA can fit into all of the major operating systems, such as macOS, Windows 10/11, iOS, Android, and Linux, something that the chatbot cannot do.

The Concept of the Node

In the world of AI, an important concept is that of the "node".

The conversation that a Digital Person generates can be viewed as the output. But what is further unique about the Digital Person is that it can pull in from other resources that it has not been initially trained on, partly because it is powered by Generative AI and also because of the nodes.

Each dataset that has been ingested into the algorithms that drive the Digital Person can be viewed as a node. So, if you had a telehealth appointment with a Digital Assistant and asked for a prescription, it would go through all five of the datasets (as represented by the nodes in the illustration) in order to provide the correct and best possible output.

The Advantages of the Digital Person

There are a number of key benefits that a Digital Person brings, and they are as follows:

1) Time Management for Employees:

It can augment your staff. For example, it is the call center that is one of the best use cases of the Digital Person. Human agents are totally inundated with phone calls and email messages, and the end results are long wait times for the end user and increased levels of frustration. The Digital Person can alleviate these problems, by being available on a 24x7x365 basis.

2) Analysis of Data:

The Digital Person also has a repository where previous conversations with end users are stored. This information can then be pulled as a reference point for future conversations with the end users, so that it can be customized and tailored.

3) Ideal for Recruitment:

With the recent round of job cuts, many people are now looking for employment. In this realm, a Digital Person can act as a human resources representative and conduct an online interview with a candidate. Also, it can scan through resumes very quickly and provide feedback to the human recruiters as to which candidates they should take a closer look at.

4) The Healthcare Industry:

During the COVID-19 pandemic, telehealth received a gargantuan boost. This is where a patient could have a video conference with their doctor, as opposed to an in person visit. But now, the Digital Person has become the front end here, thus relieving the doctors to attend to more serious matters. But it should be noted here that the Digital Person at this point can only handle simple telehealth appointments, not complex ones.

5) Availability:

As previously mentioned, the Digital Person can be made available on a 24x7x365 basis. So, if your business needs to have a support line that is manned all of the time, the Digital Person would be a great option to have here.

6) Use in Training Videos:

Rather than have a human being deliver the content, the Digital Person can work just as well. But since the technology is still evolving, they can only be used for simple training purposes, not complex ones, where a human being is still required. Another obstacle that needs to be further addressed here is the type of interactive questions that can be asked of the Digital Person in these videos. For instance, it will have to be trained initially on a wide range of queries, before it can provide an answer.

The Disadvantages of the Digital Person

The Digital Person also has its share of drawbacks, which are as follows:

1) Lack of Customization:
   Depending upon the platform that you use, there could be constraints on how customized you can make your Digital Person, especially for "niche" markets.
2) Lack of Understanding Complex Commands:
   A complex query can be viewed as one where the end user makes a series of requests in one sentence. Rather than breaking them down individually, the Digital Person will interpret all of them as just one large query. As a result, separate sentences have to be created for each query in order to ensure that the right outputs are computed.
3) Difficulty for Multi-Language Support:
   At the present time, the Digital Person can only support the most widely used languages, such as English and Spanish.
4) The Lack of Offline Functionality:
   If for some reason the power goes off to the server that hosts your Digital Person application, it will no longer be able to fully support 24x7x365 availability, as reviewed earlier.

Our next chapter will review key cybersecurity metrics and Key Performance Indicators (KPIs). The chapter after that will then go into the detail of the solution that we propose as to how the Digital Person and Generative AI can help to combat phishing, as detailed in the first chapter.

Notes

1 www.nvidia.com/en-us/glossary/generative-ai/

2 www.techtarget.com/whatis/definition/large-language-model-LLM

3 www.oracle.com/artificial-intelligence/generative-ai/retrieval-augmented-generation-rag

4 www.gartner.com/en/topics/generative-ai

5 www.ibm.com/topics/computer-vision

6 www.sas.com/en_us/insights/big-data/what-is-big-data.html

7 www.qualtrics.com/experience-management/customer/natural-language-understanding

8 www.qualtrics.com/experience-management/customer/natural-language-understanding

9 https://aws.amazon.com/what-is/deep-learning

10 https://medium.com/@yasindusanjeewa8/dense-vectors-in-natural-language-processing-06818dff5cd7

11 keyreply.com

12 www.fastcompany.com/90775977/what-does-it-mean-to-be-a-digital-person-and-why-would-multifamily-operators-and-residents-care#:~:text=Digital%20people%20are%20human%2Dlike,in%20lifelike%20and%20real%20conversations

13 www.techtarget.com/searchcustomerexperience/definition/chatbot

4

REVIEW OF CYBERSECURITY METRICS

An Introduction to Cybersecurity Risk Assessment

In the world of cybersecurity today, one of the most common techno-jargon terms that is being thrown about is that of "Risk". To many individuals and businesses, this specific term can have many different meanings, depending upon the situation or environment that they are in. But for the purposes of this chapter and the remainder of the book, "Risk", as it applies to cybersecurity, can be technically defined as follows:

> Cybersecurity risks relate to the loss of confidentiality, integrity, or availability of information, data, or information (or control) systems and reflect the potential adverse impacts to organizational operations (i.e., mission, functions, image, or reputation) and assets, individuals, other organizations, and the Nation.[1]

To put it in simpler terms, Cybersecurity Risk can simply reflect the downtime that a business can withstand before starting to face serious financial losses. But there are also other intangible risks that need to be taken into account, such as brand/reputational loss, and even more importantly, the loss that a business could face if they lose customers because of a security breach. According to the old saying, "It can take years to get a customer, but just seconds to lose them".

So now the bottom line is how does one exactly calculate Cybersecurity Risk? If one were to conduct a basic Google search in this regard, there are many resources one can find on how to accomplish this particular task. This is by no means an easy feat to accomplish, and

DOI: 10.1201/9781003503781-4

a lot depends upon the size of your business. For example, a smaller one may find it easier because they have fewer tangible assets, but a much larger one (such as a Fortune 500 company) may find it much more time and resource heavy, because of course they will have a lot more assets to take into consideration.

Therefore, it is always best to go with a reputable provider. Two of the best places to start would be the frameworks from the National Institute of Science and Technology (also known as "NIST") and the large wireless carrier Verizon. For an overview of the Cybersecurity Risk Assessment model available from NIST, see

http://cyberresources.solutions/genai_book/NIST_Cyber_Risk.pdf.

For an overview of the Cybersecurity Risk Assessment model from Verizon, see http://cyberresources.solutions/genai_book/Verizon_Cyber_Risk.pdf.

We have also recently co-authored a book that delves much deeper into this topic and examines the major statistical algorithms that can be used to calculate your level of cybersecurity risk. This book can be previewed at www.routledge.com/Assessing-and-Insuring-Cybersecurity-Risk/Das/p/book/9780367903077.

But whatever framework or model you and your IT security team choose to go with, the concepts of carrying out the process are virtually the same. This is outlined in the next subsection.

Conducting the Cybersecurity Risk Assessment

Here is an overview of how this can be done:

1) Examine your entire IT/network infrastructure:
   In this first step, carefully examine where you have all of your servers, email systems, databases, etc. But even more importantly, take an assessment of where all of your datasets currently reside, and what your plans for them are for the future. Given the fact that data privacy and compliance with data privacy laws (such as the GDPR, CCPA, HIPAA, etc.) are of paramount importance today, it is best that you only keep those datasets that you need for the immediate term, and

discard those that are either archived or "at rest". By doing this, you will greatly minimize your risk exposure in case your business becomes a victim of a security breach.

2) Take an inventory:

After you have taken a careful examination of what actually resides in your IT and network infrastructure, take a very careful inventory of *all of the digital and physical assets* you have in your business. It is very important that you take both into consideration; if not, your calculated level of cybersecurity risk could be greatly skewed. An exception to this rule would be if you decided to just focus your efforts upon one or the other (digital or physical). Once you have taken this inventory, then organize and categorize them in such a way that it will be easy for you and your IT security team to keep track of them.

3) Choose a ranking system:

Once you have taken an exhaustive inventory of both your digital and physical assets, you now need to decide upon a ranking system that will categorize the degree of vulnerability that these assets will fall under. In this regard, it is best to use some sort of quantitative based ranking system. For example, you could potentially choose a system that is based on a scale of 1–10. For example, the value "1" would represent the least amount of vulnerability, and a value of "10" would indicate the highest amount of vulnerability. Anything in between would of a lower, intermediate, or higher range. This can be seen in the following matrix.

RANKING (NUMERICAL VALUE)	DEGREE OF VULNERABILITY
1	Least Vulnerable
2–4	Increasing Amount of Vulnerability
5	Intermediate Level of Vulnerability
6–9	Increasing Amount of Vulnerability
10	Most Vulnerable

It is important to note that the term "vulnerability" is a very important one when conducting a Cybersecurity Risk Assessment, so therefore it needs to be technically defined, which is as follows:

A vulnerability is a weakness in an IT system that can be exploited by an attacker to deliver a successful attack. They can occur through flaws, features or user error, and attackers will look to exploit any of them, often combining one or more, to achieve their end goal.[2]

For example, if you have a digital asset or physical asset that has a numerical ranking of "1", it would mean that a cyberattacker would have a very hard time penetrating into it to deploy the malicious payload. Or it could also simply mean that this particular asset (whether it is digital or physical) is of no significant value or interest to the cyberattacker. A numerical value of "10" would signify that a digital asset or physical asset is extremely prone to being penetrated into by a cyberattacker in order to deploy the malicious payload. A prime example of this would be your database server, which would house your Personally Identifiable Information (PII) datasets.

4) Compile the list:

Once you have identified all of your digital assets and physical assets and assigned a numerical value to their degree of vulnerability, you need to then compile all of them into one list. For this purpose, it is highly recommended that you organize this particular list in a top down fashion. For example, those digital assets and physical assets with a numerical value of 10 would be at the top, and those with a numerical value of 1 would be at the bottom of the list. An example of this is illustrated in Figure 4.1:

5) Implement the controls:

Once you have compiled the list in the last section, you now need to take those digital assets and physical assets with a numerical ranking of 6 and above and decide on how you are going to protect them from a security breach. Of course, those digital assets and physical assets with a numerical ranking of 10 will need the most immediate attention. One of the best ways to fortify these kinds of assets is to deploy the right set of controls that can be associated with them. In this situation, you may need to either establish a brand new control, or simply

Figure 4.1 This is an illustration of how to rank vulnerable assets, according to their degree of severity.

upgrade an existing control so that it is fully optimized. Some examples of this are as follows:

- Authentication:
  On your database server, you may have set up Two Factor Authentication (also known as "2FA"). If you have identified this asset with a numerical ranking of 6 or higher, you can then deploy what is known as Multifactor Authentication (also known as "MFA"). This is where you would deploy at least three or more differing forms of authentication, in order to fully confirm the identity of the end user trying to gain access to the database server.
- Patches:
  You may have discovered in your Risk Assessment Study that your IT security team does not follow a regular

schedule of applying software updates and patches (even including firmware) to your servers. Thus, this will also leave them highly vulnerable. To counter this, you can not only implement a set of practices for this, but also establish a regular schedule for doing so.

In the next sections, we turn our attention to those specific Cybersecurity Metrics and Key Performance Indicators (also known as KPIs) that have a strong influence on your total level of Cybersecurity Risk. We will be focusing on two key ones in Chapter 5, as we propose our Generative AI and phishing solution.

An Introduction to Cybersecurity Metrics

In any kind of market application, industry, or position, having the ability to gauge an event, product, or service is a must, in order to make sure that you are receiving a positive return on investment (also known as ROI) on it. If you are not, then you are most likely receiving a negative ROI, and in this case you have one of two choices:

- Terminate the event, product, or service.
- Carefully analyze why a negative ROI is being achieved, and think of new ideas and strategies as to how to achieve a positive ROI over a pre-established period of time.

Of course, depending once again on the industry that your company is in, there could be many, perhaps even hundreds, of pre-established metrics you could choose from that are most relevant to your event, product, or service. The bottom line is that you need to have a "pulse" on what you are delivering, and by using metrics, this is one of the best ways to do this.

In the world of cybersecurity, this could not be truer. Given how quickly things are advancing here, a CISO and their respective IT security team need to know quickly how effective their work is in terms of not only fortifying the lines of defense for their business, but also for thwarting the present threat variants that are lurking in the IT and network infrastructure, or those that could potentially be.

Later in this chapter, we will take a much deeper dive into the various Cybersecurity Metrics that are currently available. We will not take a look at each and every one of them, as that could be an entire book on its own. But rather, we will review the ones that are most important for a business, and that have relevance to the Generative AI and phishing solution that we will be proposing in Chapter 5.

But to give you an idea of just how relevant metrics are in cybersecurity today, consider these:

- They can give insight into various threat patterns, and even extrapolate future ones as well, based on existing data.
- They can be used to gauge the effectiveness of Incident Response, Disaster Recovery, and Businesses Continuity Plans as they are rehearsed on a regular basis.
- As reviewed in the last subsection of this chapter, Cybersecurity Metrics can be especially useful in conducting a Risk Assessment Study, in order to determine the degree of vulnerability in each and every digital asset and physical asset.
- They can reflect the robustness and effectiveness of both the cybersecurity initiatives that have taken place and the security tools that are in place, along the lines of defense. Typically, this would include the firewalls, routers, network intrusion devices, etc. For example, if any of these devices are not coming up to par with the pre-established metric this is an indication that the device needs to be further optimized, as quickly as possible.
- They also reflect the level of cyber resilience that a company has. This can be technically defined as follows:

Cyber resilience refers to an organization's ability to identify, respond, and recover swiftly from an IT security incident. Building cyber resilience includes making a risk-focused plan that assumes the business will at some point face a breach or an attack.[3]

In other words, this means how quickly mission critical operations can be restored after being impacted by a security breach. But "quickness" is reflected in the Cybersecurity Metrics that are associated with it. Without some sort of quantitative measure, the term "quickness" can be a very subjective and qualitative term.

- Cybersecurity Metrics also demonstrate how much a company needs to improve its current Cybersecurity Posture in order to detect and evade the threat variants of tomorrow.

The Difference Between IT Security Metrics

You may have heard the terms Cybersecurity Metrics and IT Security Metrics; they overlap in certain areas, but also differ. For instance, they both deal with the overall protection of the business. But in terms of cybersecurity, the metrics typically reflect the degree of vulnerability of the digital assets and the physical assets, and the total amount of time it can take to detect, respond to, and contain any signs of anomalous or malicious behavior.

With regards to IT security, the metrics are concerned with the entire IT and network infrastructure that underlies the whole business, and in some ways, cybersecurity can be considered to be a subset of IT security. For example, to illustrate these fine differences, it is typically the IT security team that will take care of the provision and deployment of new company devices to the employees.

But it is then up to the cybersecurity team to make sure that all necessary security protocols are set up on these devices and that employees are instructed as to what constitutes acceptable and unacceptable use of them. Also, this team will be primarily responsible for making sure that all of the devices (both current and new ones) are also kept up to date with the latest software patches and updates, even including the firmware.

The Importance of Cybersecurity Metrics

In the last section, we took a close look at why Cybersecurity Metrics matter so much in today's threat environment. In this section, we now take an equally close look at why *they are especially important*. Here are the key reasons why:

1) They give the ability to make decisions:
   Cybersecurity Metrics allow the CISO and their IT security team not only to gauge what is happening right now, but

also to monitor trends of what has happened in the past. By having this kind of historical data, various statistical trends can be plotted which can clearly show how well a business's Cybersecurity Posture has performed or by how much it has declined over a period of time. The good news here is that with Generative AI, these trends can be plotted very quickly, and on demand. By knowing and seeing these kinds of trends, the CISO and their IT security team will be able to make well informed decisions, and even substantiate their findings to members of the C-suite. It will also enable well thought out plans to be created as well.

2) They are an effective communications tool:

In a business, it is important for everybody to fully understand what is happening in terms of the cyberthreat landscape. Unfortunately, this is not a trend that is happening in the majority of companies right now, but nevertheless, it is an important function that needs to be done. But the main issue here is that not everybody can speak the same "language of cybersecurity". For example, the members of the IT security team will know every nuance of a malicious payload, but all of these granular details will not matter to, say, the marketing department of the business. Therefore, by having a set of key Cybersecurity Metrics defined and updated on a continual basis, this will give a vehicle to serve as a "common denominator" which all key stakeholders can understand. For example, if you can explain that "X" number of employees fell prey to a mock phishing attack over a period of time, then this will help all employees of a business to understand that the levels of cyber hygiene need to be improved greatly. Also, the C-suite will be far better able to understand a Cybersecurity Metric and what it could mean to the bottom line.

3) They show progress:

Probably the one area in which metrics are used the most is for sales. For example, how well a salesperson is doing is typically judged by whether they meet their quota or not. This same principle can also be applied to the IT security team. Probably the two biggest metrics here will be the "Mean Time

To Detect" (also known as the "MTTD") and the "Mean Time To Respond" (also known as the "MTTR"). As their names imply, these two key Cybersecurity Metrics reflect how well the IT security team can detect and respond to a threat variant. In these specific cases, the lower the number is, the better the IT security team is at these two primary functions. But of course, the higher these two metrics are, the worse the IT security team is at performing them. This will give the CISO the first indicators that changes need to be made, for example, with the network security tools that are being used, or in terms of providing more education and training to the IT security team.

4) Data protection:

As has been mentioned throughout this book, some of the major issues of today relate not only to data privacy, but also to making sure that you are keeping those datasets safe as well. By deploying a key set of Cybersecurity Metrics here, you will know how well they are being protected. For example, a key metric here would be keeping track of how often software patches and updates are being deployed on your database server. If the Cybersecurity Metrics reflect that they are not being performed on the prescribed schedule, then this will be an area that will need immediate attention to rectify. Also, by keeping a key set of Cybersecurity Metrics here as well, this will help you to determine if the controls you have in place are effective or not, which in turn will help you comply with the data privacy laws GDPR, CCPA, HIPAA, etc.

5) Keep ahead of the industry:

Most likely, the industry that your business is in already has certain benchmarks that are deemed to be what constitutes a satisfactory level of cyber hygiene. By using Cybersecurity Metrics, you can see how effective your Cybersecurity Posture is in comparison with your industry peers. If the metrics are deemed to be less favorable for any reason, then this is a very strong indication that you and your IT security team have to take corrective actions immediately, so that you can catch up or even stay ahead.

6) Optimization:

As alluded to earlier in this book, once you have determined where all of your most vulnerable digital assets and physical assets are, you then need to either deploy a new set of controls, or upgrade any existing ones that are in place. But over the course of time, you will need to know about the performance of these controls. By establishing an appropriate set of cybersecurity controls here, you will get a first indication of this and also whether any of them need to be further optimized. Also, by having these in place, you will be able to relay the effectiveness of your cybersecurity efforts and initiatives not only to the C-suite but also to the board of directors in an efficient manner that can be understood by all.

What Are Cybersecurity Metrics and Key Performance Indicators?

There is often a good deal of confusion as to what a Cybersecurity Metric is when compared to a Key Performance Indicator (also known as a "KPI"). For the purposes of this book, a Cybersecurity Metric can be defined as follows:

Cybersecurity metrics are bits of data that a company tracks on a day-to-day basis. They are business-as-usual data that offer value but may or may not drive decisions.[4]

The key difference between Cybersecurity Metrics and Key Performance Indicators is that the former are pieces of data and computed values that show how a certain process is working. For example, over a period of one week, how well has your IT security team effectively triaged all of the legitimate warnings and alerts that have come in? But with the latter, this reflects how well an overall objective or goal is being met. For example, as discussed earlier, a good example of this is how your Cybersecurity Posture stands in comparison with others in the industry. This is not something that should be measured on a day to day basis, but rather examining this on a quarterly basis would be far more effective.

In other words, the Cybersecurity Metrics reflect what happens on a continual basis, and the Key Performance Indicators (KPIs) demonstrate what is happening over a certain period of time and are usually much longer term in nature.

Although these two are equally important, for the remainder of this book we will be examining just Cybersecurity Metrics.

The Four Categories of Cybersecurity Metrics

Although there are many Cybersecurity Metrics (as we will see later in this chapter), they all fall under four major groupings, which are as follows:

1) The Vulnerability Assessment Metrics:

   Although we have reviewed the concept of vulnerabilities as they relate to digital assets and physical assets, it can also be associated with the following:

   • The total number of systems, devices, virtual machines, etc. that still need to be patched.
   • Based upon conducting a Vulnerability Scan, the total number of network ports that are still open and not being used.
   • The total number of devices that still need to be configured up to the security requirements.

2) The Attack Detection Metrics:

   These are the Cybersecurity Metrics that reflect the time it takes for a company to detect, respond, and contain a threat variant. As stated earlier, the two best metrics here are the Mean Time To Detect and the Mean Time To Respond.

3) The Compliance Metrics:

   These are the Cybersecurity Metrics that reflect how well a business is complying with the relevant regulations and standards. Examples of this include the following:

   • The total number of security controls that have been established for each of the digital assets and physical assets.
   • The total number of security policies that are in place.
   • The total number of security awareness training sessions that have been delivered, say, on a quarterly basis.

4) The Performance Metrics:

These Cybersecurity Metrics reflect just how effective a business's overall initiatives are and if a positive return on investment (ROI) is being realized. Examples of these include the following:

- The total number of security incidents that were responded to.
- What the costs were if a security breach actually happened.
- The returns that have been gained or lost from spending, such as investing in newer security tools and technologies.

The Use Cases for Cybersecurity Metrics

There are also five key use cases for Cybersecurity Metrics, which are as follows:

1) Accountability:

By having Cybersecurity Metrics, key decisions can be made quickly. For example, if the level of cyber hygiene is still deemed to be poor among employees, then a decision needs to be made about whether the security awareness training programs should be changed or further enhanced. It also can act as accountability measure. For example, if the Cybersecurity Metrics reflect the fact that the IT security team is still too slow to respond to and contain a threat variant, then the CISO can hold them directly accountable for this.

2) Objectivity:

When establishing the set of Cybersecurity Metrics, as far as possible, it is very important that they are quantitative based. Of course, there will always be qualitative based ones, but by having hard concrete numbers, this will eliminate any chances of bias. Thus, you can be assured that any decisions you make based upon the Cybersecurity Metrics will be objectively based.

3) Efficiency:

With a good set of Cybersecurity Metrics in place, anything out of the ordinary can be detected quickly and the appropriate corrections made. For example, if a log from a network security device shows an unusual number of attempted login attempts, then the device in question can be immediately isolated and examined closely to see what really happened.

4) Holism:

It is important to note that a key benefit of Cybersecurity Metrics is that they take into account all of the various facets and departments of a business; they do not just apply to the IT department. For example, data protection also includes the datasets that the finance and accounting departments hold. So, the controls that are implemented will not just protect what the IT department has, they will also at the same time protect the finance and accounting departments as well. For example, as described throughout this book, the Risk Assessment Study examines the vulnerabilities of *the digital assets and the physical assets throughout the entire business, not just a certain department or division.*

Good Versus Bad Cybersecurity Metrics and Associated Challenges

There are three criteria that define what a good Cybersecurity Metric is, and they are as follows:

1) It must be definable:

Whichever set of metrics you and your IT security team choose to implement, they must be definable. This simply means that they must yield a result that is measurable and that can be used as a frame of reference for future improvement. A great example of this is the Mean Time To Detect. It takes on average seven months for a company to detect a threat or even that a malicious payload is present in the IT and network infrastructure. Of course, this is a completely unfathomable and unreasonable time frame. Therefore, you may want to bring this metric down to, say, three months. After a period of time, you then take a reading of this metric again, to see whether the time to detect has improved or not. If it has not, then you know that drastic corrective actions must be taken quickly. This is what is meant by "definable".

2) It must be comprehensive:

The chosen Cybersecurity Metrics must also cover a wide spectrum. For example, it is not good practice to just have metrics that reflect only what is happening to one department of a business. Rather, they must reflect all of them. For example, with the Mean Time To Detect metric, this should reflect any threat variant that can impact any department within the business. For instance, a malicious payload will not just impact the IT department, it will affect all departments. In this regard, the metric must also be broad enough in scope to reflect this requirement. This is what is meant by "comprehensive".

3) It must be comparable:

Along with the other two key criteria, the chosen Cybersecurity Metrics must be relatable to other similar metrics. For example, with the Mean Time To Detect metric, once you have calculated it for your business, then compare it with what the figure is for your overall industry. For example, if you have computed the Mean Time To Detect for your business to be three months, and your industry standard is one month, then you will know immediately that, once again, corrective actions must be taken. This is what is meant by "comparable".

A Methodology for Choosing the Cybersecurity Metrics

It is important to note that while you and your IT security team choose the Cybersecurity Metrics that are most relevant for your business, you should not simply do it haphazardly. Rather, there must be a defined methodology for doing this, and an example of this is shown in Figure 4.2:

The Cybersecurity Metrics

Now that we have provided a solid overview of what Cybersecurity Metrics are and why they are relevant as well as important, in this section we now examine the top metrics that you should consider deploying and implementing in your business.

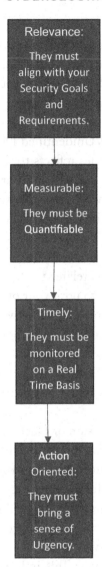

Figure 4.2   A methodology in how to choose the right Cybersecurity Metrics.

1) Preparedness:
   This grouping of metrics reflects how ready your business is to handle a security breach, should it happen. Key metrics here are:
   • Software Updates/Patches: This measures the frequency of how often you apply the necessary patches and upgrades.

- Compliance: This relates more to data protection and reflects how optimized your controls are for your databases.
- Vulnerabilities that are High Risk: This is done in the Risk Assessment Study, where you identify those digital assets and physical assets that are deemed to be "highly vulnerable".

2) Number of Identified/Unidentified Devices:
This grouping of metrics reflects the total number of devices (both physical and virtual) that are connected and not connected to your network infrastructure. Key metrics here are:

- Count of Devices: This relates to the total number of devices that are being used and *that are not connected to your own network but are connected somewhere else.*
- Inventory Log: This relates to the total number of devices that are connected, to both your own network and external ones (such as the home based networks of remote workers).
- Protocols: This indicates whether all of the necessary security measures are installed on each and every device. This is especially relevant to wireless devices. This is a metric that should be calculated when devices are beginning the provisioning process.

3) Total Number of Intrusion or Hacking Attempts:
This grouping of metrics reflects the total number of times that a cyberattacker has penetrated into your business, whether or not they were successful. Key metrics here are:

- Total Number of Breaches: This represents the total number of times that your business has been impacted by an actual threat variant, if any.
- Analysis of Frequency: This indicates the total number of *unsuccessful attempts that have been made by cyberattackers to penetrate into your IT and network infrastructure.* A good example of this is the total number of unsuccessful login attempts into a particular device.
- Identification of Source: This is where you try to determine the source of a cyberattack. It is also technically known as "attribution". This metric is actually very difficult to gauge, especially if you are dealing with nation-state threat actors.

4) Data Exfiltration Effectiveness:

This grouping of metrics reflects how effective your controls are in protecting your databases and in mitigating the risk of the datasets being taken out maliciously, which is technically known as "exfiltration". Key metrics here are:

- Incident Prevention: This is a mathematical ratio, in which the numerator is the number of data exfiltration attempts that have been successfully thwarted, and the denominator is the total number of attempts to break into your databases, whether successful or not.

- Response Time: This is the total amount of time that it takes your IT security team to respond to a data exfiltration attempt. It is important to note that this metric is *exclusive to this, and does not relate to any other threat variants.*

- False Positives: This reflects the total number of false warnings and alerts that are presented to the IT security team. If there are too many of them, this can lead to a phenomenon called "alert fatigue".

5) The Mean Time Between Failures:

This is also known as the "MTBF". This grouping of metrics reflects the downtime that is experienced by your business between two consecutive events in which there has been some sort of failure in your IT and network infrastructure. Key metrics here are:

- Degree of Reliability: This demonstrates the total cyber resilience of your IT and network infrastructure. The larger the number is, the more robust this metric is.

- Maintenance That Can Be Predicted: This reflects how often the devices in your IT and network infrastructure need to be fixed, based upon past and historical data.

- Predictive Trends: This is a more long term metric, and a longer trend line with few spikes in between indicates a rather robust IT and network infrastructure.

6) The Mean Time To Detect:

This is also known as the "MTTD", and this grouping of metrics demonstrates how long it takes for your IT security team to respond to a threat variant, as reviewed throughout this book. Key metrics here are:

- Detection of Efficiency: This indicates how efficient your IT security team is in detecting a threat variant.
- Response Strategies: This reflects the steps you plan to take to reduce the overall MTTD metric.
- Benchmarking With Industry Standards: This is where you take the MTTD that you have computed for your business and compare it to your industry wide MTTD, as reviewed throughout this chapter.

7) The Mean Time To Acknowledge:

This is also known as the "MTTA". This is the total amount of time that it takes for your IT security to inform other key stakeholders in your company that it has indeed been impacted by a threat variant. Key metrics here are:

- Readiness of Response: This indicates how quickly you and your IT security team can respond to a threat variant on a real-time basis.
- Documentation Compliance: This reflects the total number of times that you rehearse your Incident Response/Disaster Recovery/Business Continuity Plans, and how often you keep these sets of documentation updated.
- Improvement of Procedures: This shows any time delays that have been experienced in the MTTA metric. From here, you and your IT security team will need to come up with a refined set of procedures to shorten this time frame.

8) The Mean Time To Contain:

This is also known as the "MTTC". This grouping of metrics reflects the degree to which your IT security can contain, or isolate, a threat variant before it spreads further throughout your IT and network infrastructure. Key metrics here are:

- Efficiency of Containment: This reflects how efficient your team is in containing a threat variant. A key variable here is the total amount of time that it takes to do this.
- Evaluation of Process: This indicates how optimized your threat variant containment procedures are.

- Consistency in Containment: This demonstrates how uniform your IT security team is in containing a threat variant.
- Improvement of Procedures: Your business also needs to have a set of documented containment procedures, and this metric reflects how often you practice and update this particular set of documents.

9) The Mean Time To Resolve:

This is also known as the "MTTR". This grouping of metrics reflects how long it takes for you and your IT security team to actually understand what the threat variant is, if it has actually impacted your business. Key metrics here are:

- The Efficiency of Resolution: This reflects the total amount of time it takes for your IT security team to fully resolve the threat variant. There may be no particular benchmark for this metric, as this time can vary for each and every kind of threat variant.
- Evaluation of Process: This indicates how optimized your threat variant resolution procedures are.
- Improvement of Procedures: Your business also needs to have a set of documented resolution procedures, and this metric reflects how often you practice and update this particular set of documents.
- Analysis of Trends: This reflects the overall trends and patterns in the total amount of time it takes to resolve a threat variant. Although this can be subjective, the shorter the gap between spikes in unusual network traffic patterns the better, as this is indicative that your IT security team possesses the knowledge and skills needed to fully resolve threat variants in a very short amount of time.

10) The Mean Time To Recovery:

This is also known as the "MTTR". This grouping of metrics reflects how long it takes for your business to recover from the impact of a threat variant. Key metrics here are:

- The Efficiency of Recovery: This reflects how efficiently your business can recover from any kind of security breach.

This metric is especially critical if you have been affected by a ransomware attack.

- Analysis of History: This reflects the overall trends and patterns in the total amount of time it takes to resolve a threat variant. By examining the time periods that are associated with the spikes, you can fine tune and optimize your Incident Response/Disaster Recovery/Business Continuity Plans even more.

- Level of Preparedness: This indicates how proactive you and your IT security team are in getting your business back up and running again. There are two considerations that need to be taken into account here:

*The Level of Preparedness in restoring mission critical operations. This relates directly to Incident Response.
*The Level of Preparedness in restoring all the business processes to a normal state, as they were before the security breach occurred. This relates directly to Disaster Recovery and Business Continuity.

- Improvement of Procedures: This measures how often (or the frequency at which) you update your Incident Response/Disaster Recovery/Business Continuity Plans, even after you have practiced them, and discovered any lessons learned.

- The Analysis of Impact: This reflects the total damage that your business has suffered as a result of a security breach. There are two key considerations here, which are as follows:

*The direct financial loss to the bottom line as a result of the security breach.
*The indirect costs. These are more subjective and qualitative to determine. Examples include lost customers, brand/reputation damage, and legal actions pertaining to the loss of datasets (especially those related to Personally Identifiable Information [PII]).

11) The Time for Deployment of Software Patches and Upgrades: A critical aspect of cybersecurity today is making sure that all of your systems, devices, servers, workstations, etc. are updated

with the necessary patches and upgrades that relate to all of the software components in them. These need to be deployed in both your physical and virtual environments, and even a hybrid one if you have that (this is where you have part of your infrastructure both in the Cloud and On Premises). Thus, the critical Cybersecurity Metric that becomes of paramount importance is what is known as the "Days To Patch", also known as the "DTP".

To calculate this particular Cybersecurity Metric, take the total number of vulnerabilities that you have patched (this will become the numerator) and divide it by the total number of vulnerabilities that you have identified and that have not been patched (this will become the denominator). This will of course become a percentage, and a higher percentage indicates that you and your IT security team are deploying and applying the software patches and upgrades on a timely basis. But if the number is lower, then this simply reflects the fact that you are not following a regular regimen in this regard and that you are leaving your IT and network infrastructure at a much graver risk of being impacted by a security breach.

This particular Cybersecurity Metric will also tell you two more things:
- How long it takes your IT security team to deploy and apply the software patches and upgrades.
- It will also give you a strong benchmark in how to maintain a set of best practices and standards in securing your IT and network infrastructure.

12) The Cybersecurity Awareness Training:
Providing training sessions for your employees on how to maintain the proper levels of cyber hygiene is of paramount importance today. This kind of training has to be specific to the target audience (for example, if you are trying to provide security awareness training for employees of the finance department, then it should be geared to how they can avoid phishing attacks that could involve a fake invoice asking for a large amount of money to be wired). Also, the training needs to be geared towards employees who work remotely, on site,

and in a hybrid way. Finally, the training that you provide must be effective, so that the audience will literally, using the old proverb, "Practice What You Preach". This, for the most part, can be achieved by using the concepts of what is known as "gamification".

To this effect, there are three key metrics that are most relevant:

- Training Coverage: This reflects whether you are providing enough training to all employees in your business, ranging all the way from the C-suite to the administrative assistants.
- Improvement of Procedures: Your business also needs to have a set of documented security awareness training procedures, and this metric reflects how often you practice and update this particular set of documents.
- Engagement: This reflects how effective your audience feels your training was. This can be best measured by offering them a short, numerically based survey to fill out, with the option to leave text based answers as well.
- Integration: This metric reflects how well you "blend" in your audience together. For example, is one part of it being favored more so than the other? Obviously, this is something that you do not want to happen, and it should be avoided at all costs. The only way you will know this is by getting feedback, as mentioned earlier.
- Other Relevant KPIs and Metrics: There are others that are equally important here, and they are as follows:

*The quantifiable rates of engagement.

*How often you provide security awareness training for your employees (a good rule of thumb here is at least once a quarter, at minimum).

*How often you test your audience: For example, do you provide the tests during the security awareness training, or do you do it a brief period of time after it has ended?

*How often your employees fall prey to a mock attack. For example, after a brief period of time, if you launch a mock phishing attack, how many of your employees actually fall for this?

13) The Total Number of Cybersecurity Incidents That Have Been Reported:

As its name implies, this is purely a quantitative based metric that reflects the total number of times that cybersecurity issues have been reported. But it is important to keep in mind that this also includes the following:

- The total number of incidents that have occurred but have not been responded to.
- The total number of incidents that have occurred and have been resolved.
- The total number of possible penetrations of threat variants that have not been reported but have been cited to public agencies such as OWASP, CISA, etc.
- The total number of threat variants that have been reported and cited.
- The total number of threat variants that have been reported, cited, and penetrated into your IT and network infrastructure.

14) The Access Management:

Access Management is critical to a business, as this is where you assign the rights, privileges, and permissions for each and every employee in your business. Even more critical are those that are placed at a higher level, and this is technically known as "Privileged Access Management", also referred to quite commonly as "PAM". The main metric that is of primary importance in this regard is what is known as the "User Authentication Success Rate", also referred to as the "UASR" for short.

Essentially, it measures how effective your authentication mechanisms are in confirming the identity of the individual in question. This could be either Two Factor Authentication (also known as "2FA"), or Multifactor Authentication (also known as MFA). The authentication mechanisms could range anywhere from a password to a challenge/response question to an RSA token or even biometric identification (such as fingerprint recognition or iris recognition).

This metric measures the total number of times that an employee has been successfully authenticated versus the total number of login attempts, both successful and unsuccessful. In this regard, the former becomes the numerator, and the latter becomes the denominator. The higher the percentage rate is, the more robust your authentication mechanisms are. A lower percentage can indicate that a much less robust authentication mechanism is in place, although this can also mean that there are a large number of unsuccessful login attempts, which should raise a very serious red flag that a cyberattacker is trying to penetrate through, or that an insider attack could be taking place. In this instance, a low percentage can indicate a robust mechanism.

15) The Security Policy Compliance:
This metric reflects how well all of your employees are abiding by the security policies that you and your IT security team have set forth. This may not necessarily be a quantitative based number, but rather, it could be a much more qualitative based one, as you will have to depend upon others to get feedback.

Other key metrics here include the following:

• How legally compliant your deployed controls are. Probably the most important regulations here are those that relate to data protection and privacy, and this is where the tenets and provisions of the GDPR, CPPA, IIIPAA all come into play.

• The total number of processes that you have in place in order to make sure that your employees are abiding by your security policies. Some of the best examples here include those that relate to passwords and shadow IT management (this is where employees download and use unauthorized applications in order to conduct their everyday job functions).

16) The Total Amount of Human Traffic:
This metric tracks how much human network traffic comes into a business versus that coming from "bots".

While a bot can be used for advantageous purposes, it can also be used for nefarious ones as well, such as staging a DDoS attack against a target computer or even computers. Some other key metrics that need to be taken into consideration also include:

• If there is an unusual uptick of network related activity that is coming into and out of your business. Also, another key consideration here is the time that it happens. For example, if it happens at odd hours during the night, then this could be a strong indication that your business could become the target of a massive DDoS attack.

- The total percentage of human traffic that you have (such as your employees logging into their workstations or devices) versus the total amount of automated traffic that you are witnessing.

17) The Virus Infection Monitoring:

One of the greatest fears today amongst all businesses are viruses, worms, Trojan horses, and other pieces of malicious payloads. While there is nothing new about them, they have become more covert, stealthier, and deadlier today. The primary metric that is of most concern here is called "Continuous Monitoring". This reflects the amount of time that your IT security team have devoted to the 24x7x365, real-time monitoring of your IT and network infrastructure for these types of threat variants. Equally important is the Continuous Monitoring on all of your endpoints as well. Other key metrics to take into account here include:

- The total number of times that your anti-malware/antivirus software packages, as well as your XDR and EDR solutions, scan other systems, such as the following:

  * Email clients
  * All web browsers that are being used (such as Microsoft Edge, Google Chrome, Mozilla Firefox, Apple Safari, etc.).
  * The actions (whether by human intervention or automated) that are taken by your EDR/XDR solutions and anti-malware/antivirus software packages when a threat variant has been detected.
  * The steps that are taken to contain the viruses, worms, Trojan horses, and other pieces of malicious payloads.

18) The Phishing Attack Success:

As reviewed extensively in Chapter 1, phishing, while one of the oldest forms of threat variants, still remains one of the most widely used ones. The primary metric that is of concern here is what is known as the "phishing Click Rate". It reflects the total percentage of your employees that have fallen victim to a phishing email, whether it was an intentional one (from a cyberattacker) or one that was not intentional (such as a phishing simulation attack). Anything that represents a very high click rate is indicative that your employees are merely clicking on links or malicious downloadables without thinking ahead of time if this particular message could be a phishing based one. This is then a reflection that more security awareness training needs to be given in this regard.

19) The Total Cost Per Incident:

When compared to some of the others Cybersecurity Metrics detailed thus far in this chapter, this could be one of the most important ones to consider. This particular metric reflects how much money you have lost because of a security breach. This was elaborated on earlier in this chapter, but there are also two key metrics that are of prime importance:

• What is the total cost that is involved in responding to a cyberattack?
• What is the total cost that is involved in responding when trying to resolve a cyberattack?
• What are the other total costs that are involved? These might include:
* Overtime that is needed by the employees to respond to, contain, and resolve the cyberattack.
* Lost employee productivity.
* The costs of communications with other key stakeholders and customers.
* The total costs of offering impacted customers services to restore their identity, such as free credit reporting.

20) The Total Amount of Data Volume:

Data is the lifeblood of any business today, and the amount that is collected, used, stored, and archived is growing on a daily basis. Therefore, you need a solid metric to give you an idea of how much bandwidth you are consuming in relation to this. This metric will give you this indication. Of course, the more data that your business is consuming, the more bandwidth you will need. If you have a Cloud based deployment, such as Microsoft Azure, then the scaling up process will happen automatically for you.

21) The Total Number of Improperly Configured SSL Certificates:

SSL certificates are used not only to secure your own corporate websites, but also to show others, such as prospects and customers, that your online store and presence is secure.

It also shows that a secure line of communications has been established between the sender and receiver, and vice versa. But unfortunately, many times, SSL certificates are improperly configured. This metric represents this and will give you and your IT security team every indication of which SSL certificates need to be thus discarded and replaced.

22) The Deactivation Time of a Former Employee's Login Credentials:

Once an employee leaves, or is terminated for whatever reason, it is imperative that their login credentials are deprovisioned or deactivated as quickly as possible. The longer you wait to do this, the greater the chances of an insider attack happening. Unfortunately, this is the case with many businesses today, as their IT security team tends to forget to do this very critical aspect. This particular metric reflects this, and if the deactivation time is too long, then serious and quick remediative actions need to be taken. In fact, AI can be a great tool here to do this, as it can initiate the deprovisioning process on an automatic basis.

23) The Total Number of Network Ports That Are Open:

Network ports are used quite often on a daily basis with businesses today. But very often, unused ones still remain wide open, which leaves a gaping point of entry for the cyberattacker. One of the best ways to determine which network ports have remained opened in your IT/network infrastructure is by doing a Vulnerability Scan. Once this is done, the data that you receive in the final report can be used to compile this specific metric. Over time, a trend line can thus be drawn to show if the total number of open ports actually decreases over a period of time.

24) The Access by Third Party Suppliers:

In today's world, the outsourcing of business processes to third party suppliers has become the norm. Very often, this will result in the sharing of datasets with them, and every precaution must thus be taken to fully ensure that they will be safe in another entity's hands. But the reverse of this is also true, in that the third party supplier will also need to access your IT/network infrastructure. Therefore, not only will you and your IT security team need to collect data on this, but you will also have to compile a metric on it, which is what this one is all about. Obviously, you will want to give as little access as possible, and this metric can help you and your IT security team make those kinds of decisions.

25) The Frequency of Access by Third Party Suppliers:

This metric is an extension of sorts of the last metric just reviewed. With this particular one, you are determining exactly how much and how many times your third party suppliers are accessing the digital assets in your IT/network infrastructure. They should only do so to the extent that you have prescribed in the contract that you have signed and executed with them. Further, if any more access is needed, you must give them explicit permission to do so, and only via an addendum to the original contract.

26) The Total Number of Partners With Cybersecurity:

As you start the vetting process with third party suppliers and other potential partners that you may work with, you will want to make sure that they have the same type of security policies and compliance procedures as yours. This is what this particular metric measures, and one of the best ways to use this would be to try to ascertain the level you are at and then use that for comparison with the values that you have computed for the third party suppliers and partners. The rule of thumb here is that if the numbers are about the same or higher when you compare them, then that it is a good indication that the potential third party supplier or partner observes the same high standards that you do. But if the comparison yields values that are any lower, or not equal with one another, then that should be a red flag that any potential relationship should be reviewed again and scrutinized.

27) The Total Number of Privileged Access Accounts:

This is also commonly referred to as "Privileged Access Management", or "PAM" for short. This is where you and your IT security team have assigned higher than normal privileges to those with more senior roles at your business. Examples of these include the titles of network administrator, database administrator, project manager, CIO, CISO, CTO, etc. But the management of these is where most businesses are lacking today. Here are some typical instances of this:

- Not deprovisioning Privileged Access accounts as soon as they are no longer needed. Once again, this could be because an employee leaves your business, or a project has ended and thus these specific login credentials are no longer needed.
- The over-assignment of rights, privileges, and permissions. For example, assigning a network administrator title database administrator privileges when it is not needed (unless a specific project calls for this overlap).
- Keeping the same profiles, rights, permissions, and privileges for the Privileged Access accounts. For example, keeping the same profile for a network administrator Privileged Access account without updating or changing it over time. As a result, these kinds of accounts can become "stale" and even weaken, thus making it much easier for the cyberattacker to penetrate into the system.

Given these scenarios, it is thus necessary to have a metric that can reflect all of this, so that you and your IT security team can keep track of these Privileged Access accounts. Today, the cyberattacker is primarily aiming for these kinds of escalated rights, privileges, and permissions. The reason for this is that if these kinds of credentials can be exfiltrated, the cyberattacker will be able to get covert access to your mission critical assets in a much quicker way and even laterally across your entire IT/network infrastructure.

Finally, in summary, probably the five most important Cybersecurity Metrics for your business are illustrated in Figure 4.3:

As this chapter has reviewed, there are many Cybersecurity Metrics that your business can choose from. However, it is imperative that you do not try to follow all of them. Doing so will not only drain the resources that you have, but it could also give you a false sense of security. Or worse still, it could even give you and your IT security team a deep sense of confusion if all of them are followed.

Possibly one of the most effective ways of figuring out what will work best for your business is to first take a close review of your IT Security Policies. Determine if they are still good to use or if they need to have any kind of upgrades in order to reflect the current cyberthreat landscape. Once you have been through this process, then you can filter through the list in this chapter and determine which ones will best reflect those IT Security Policies.

In the next chapter, we will propose a solution that utilizes a combination of traditional cybersecurity technologies and Generative AI in an effort to combat phishing attacks. It is even possible that you can make use of this proposed solution, at least on a theoretical basis, to launch simulated exercises for mock phishing attacks in order to test the cyber hygiene of your employees. It even makes use of the Digital Person as part of the core solution.

As a summary, so far in this book, we have covered the following:

- What phishing is all about.
- Artificial Intelligence.
- Machine Learning.
- Neural Networks.
- Natural Language Processing.
- Generative AI.
- The Digital Person.
- The top Cybersecurity Metrics.

Figure 4.3 These are deemed to be the most important of the Cybersecurity Metrics.

Notes

1 https://csrc.nist.gov/glossary/term/cybersecurity_risk
2 www.ncsc.gov.uk/collection/vulnerability-management/understanding-vulnerabilities
3 www.cisco.com/c/en/us/solutions/hybrid-work/what-is-cyber-resilience.html
4 https://cybertalents.com/blog/top-15-cybersecurity-metrics-and-kpis-for-better-security

5

CONCLUSIONS

Introduction

So far in this book, we have extensively reviewed phishing, Artificial Intelligence, Machine Learning, Neural Networks, Generative AI, Natural Language Processing, the Digital Person, and an entire plethora of key Cybersecurity Metrics that are important to any business. Now, in this chapter we review a solution, at least on a theoretical basis, as to how all of this can come together to help mitigate the chances of a phishing attack affecting your business. But first, it is important to review in a little bit more detail what Privileged Access Management (PAM) is about.

A Brief Review of Privileged Access Management

As has been alluded to throughout this book, and especially in the last chapter, Privileged Access Management (also known more commonly as "PAM") is that part of the field of Identity and Access Management (also known as "IAM") that deals with the higher levels of rights, permissions, and privileges that are given to more senior titles, such as network administrators, CISOs, database administrators, project managers, etc.

Examples of Privileged Access Management from the human standpoint include the following:

1) The Super User Account:
   This is the most powerful of all the rights, privileges, and permissions that can be assigned to anybody. This kind of access grants reach to just about every component of the IT and network infrastructure within the confines of a business.

2) The Domain Access Account:

This is where the appropriate rights, permissions, and privileges are assigned, typically to network administrators, for the configuration, deployment, and maintenance of all of the devices that are in the network infrastructure or in a particular domain. This is where the phrase "Keys to the IT Kingdom" is most often used.

3) The Secure Sockets Shell Key Account:

This is also commonly referred to as "SSH". This is a kind of specialized account where the network administrator can gain root access to all of the devices, workstations, and servers in an IT and network infrastructure. It is important to note that the term "root" refers to the account that, by default, has access to all of the commands and files in a Linux/UNIX based environment. This particular term is also used in Windows and macOS environments as well, but not nearly as commonly.

4) The Emergency Account:

This type of account can be created immediately, whenever the need for it arises. For example, it can be deployed if your business has been impacted by a natural disaster or even a cyberattack. It is important to note that this is only a very temporary kind of account, and it is used primarily for Incident Response and Disaster Recovery purposes.

5) The Privileged Business User Account:

This is a kind of account that is also created on a temporary basis, but is often used by contractors (short or long term) or third party suppliers. A very special eye has to be kept on these kinds of accounts, and they must be completely deleted at the end of a project or when services are no longer needed.

Examples of Privileged Access Management from the non-human standpoint include the following:

1) The Application Account:

This is used for a specific software application or operating system that needs to be deployed, configured, and maintained.

2) The Service Account:

This is a special type of account that is used to provide unexpected maintenance to a software application or operating system.

3) The Secret/SSH Key:

This is the same kind of account as the human one just reviewed, but it is used by an AI system if the processes are automated.

The Obstacles With Privileged Access Accounts

Just like anything else that is technology-related, these kinds of accounts are also fraught with several challenges, which are as follows:

1) The Management of Accounts:

This is an area that poses the greatest challenge. At the present time, most of these kinds of accounts are managed with human intervention, causing a great deal of errors to occur, such as not deprovisioning or deleting accounts when they are no longer needed.

2) The Tracking of Activity:

At the present time, many businesses use different and disparate tools to keep track of Privileged Access account activity. Many of them do not use a centralized monitoring service, which causes a great deal of error as well, especially in the way of discrepancies.

3) The Analysis of Threats:

It is still quite difficult for businesses to ascertain if there are any threats that are being posed to Privileged Access accounts. To help alleviate this issue, AI is starting not only to filter for false positives, but also to report the legitimate warnings and alerts to the IT security team for triaging and remediation.

4) Giving the Appropriate Amount of Access:

Organizations are still struggling with how to assign exactly the required amounts of rights, privileges, and permissions to the end users. Most likely too much is being given out in this regard, thus not following the concept of "least privilege", which is so very important.

5) Attacks on Domain Controllers:
   If a Privileged Access account has been compromised, this can lead to a large attack on the Kerberos protocol. This can be technically defined as follows:

   It is a way for attackers to obtain credentials for Active Directory accounts, and then leverage those credentials to steal data.[1]

   Put in simpler terms, the Kerberos protocol makes use of "digital tickets" in order to confirm the authentication of an end user wishing to gain access to shared resources.

Best Practices for Privileged Access Accounts

To help alleviate the challenges that were posed in the last subsection, a number of best practices are recommended, which are as follows:

1) Deploy MFA:
   As has been mentioned throughout this book, this is an acronym that stands for "Multifactor Authentication". This is where two or more layers of authentication mechanisms are used in order to confirm the identity of an end user. It is important to note that these must be different controls, such as a password, an RSA token, a challenge/response question or even a biometric modality.
2) Deploy Automation:
   Since there is still so much human error that is involved with the governing of Privileged Access accounts, it is highly recommended to use an AI based system to automate most, if not all, of the process. For example, this will greatly reduce the error of not deprovisioning or deleting these kinds of accounts when they are no longer needed.
3) Do Not Assign to Endpoints:
   In this regard, it is imperative that you do not assign any kind of Privileged Access to employees who make heavy usage of wireless devices. The primary reason for this is that if an unsecure wireless network connection is used, the cyberattacker can easily access these higher level permissions,

rights, and privileges and quickly infiltrate your IT and network infrastructure.

4) Create Baselines:

This is where you create a trend of what is considered to be "normal activity". Any deviations from this should be considered as "abnormal activity", especially when it comes to the Privileged Access accounts. Of course, this can be a very laborious and time consuming task to do on a manual basis, and therefore it is highly recommended that you should make use of AI in this regard to help automate the process and to filter out, once again, the false positives.

5) Use JIT:

This is an acronym that stands for "Just In Time" access. Essentially, rather than keeping a master Privileged Access account lingering for a long time, you can provision it just when it is needed. A technical definition of this is as follows:

Just-in-time (JIT) access provisioning is a security practice that grants users, processes, applications, and systems an appropriate level of access for a limited amount of time, as needed to complete necessary tasks. As a part of the Identity and Access Management (IAM), the Just-in-Time authentication practice ensures resources are available as they're required.[2]

Another key benefit of using Just In Time access is that the end user will be given access to just the right mix of resources, thus strictly observing the concept of "least privilege".

6) Strictly Observe RBAC:

This is an acronym that stands for "Role-Based Access Control". As reviewed in the last chapter, this is where you assign specific rights, privileges, and permissions to an end user based on their job title and the daily roles that they perform. This same concept also holds true for the Privileged Access accounts. For example, you would not give the same sets of rights, permissions, and privileges to a project manager as you would to a network administrator.

An Overview of the Proposed Solution

Now that we have provided a solid grounding in Privileged Access Management, one of the key takeaways here is that these kinds and types of accounts are a prime target for the cyberattacker. The primary reason for this is that since there are super user rights, permissions, and privileges that are associated with these kinds of accounts, a cyberattacker, once they steal the confidential information and data that resides in them, can launch all sorts of sophisticated phishing attacks which include the following:

- Ransomware.
- Social Engineering Attacks.
- Extortion Style Attacks.
- Business Email Compromise (this is where a fake invoice is sent via email, putting a sense of urgency in the body of the email message).
- Spear phishing (this is where a specific victim is targeted, after the cyberattacker has built up a profile of them, primarily through the use of social media accounts).
- Smishing and Vishing (this is where phishing like text messages and voice messages are delivered to the victim).
- Whaling (this is where high ranking managers in a business are targeted, such as those in the C-suite).

In our proposed solution, there are only two key metrics that we will be looking at, and which are probably some of the most important ones. As reviewed in the last chapter, they are as follows:

1) The Mean Time to Detect:
   This is how long it takes for the IT security team to actually detect that a phishing attack is underway. This is also known as the "MTTD".
2) The Mean Time to Respond:
   This is how long it takes for the IT security team to respond to an actual phishing attack. This is also known as the "MTTR".

Of course, there are other Cybersecurity Metrics that could also be used, but for simplicity's sake, only these will be the point of focus. As mentioned earlier in this book, it takes an average of seven months for a threat (such as a phishing attack) to actually be detected and responded to. One of the primary objectives of our proposed solution is to bring this time down to a matter of just hours. It is also important to keep in mind that our proposed solution is still theoretical in nature. In the next sections, we provide the details of it.

The Components of the Proposed Solution

There will be individual components to our proposed solution, but they will all be integrated together into one cohesive unit. They are as follows:

1) An AI Driven Tool for Filtering.
2) A SIEM.
3) The Digital Person.
4) A Holistic Cyber Platform.
5) The Privileged Access Management Server.

They will now be examined in more detail:

- The Filtering Tool:
  In today's world, IT security teams are totally inundated with many alerts and warnings that are delivered to them from the network security tools, such as the routers, firewalls, network intrusion devices, etc. This problem gets compounded if the products and tools used are from many different vendors. The other problem here is that whatever is presented to the IT security team may turn out to be negative, and these are technically known as "false positives". As a result, this adds even more strain as it is necessary to figure out what is real and what is not. With the time that is being spent on this, the real threat variants often get ignored, thus putting the business at even graver risk. As was mentioned earlier in this book, this can lead to a phenomenon called "alert fatigue". In order to cure this problem, the first proposed component of our proposed solution will be a tool that can filter out these false positives and present only those legitimate threats and warnings to the IT security team so that they can be triaged and responded to in a quick fashion. To do this kind of task on a real-time

basis, an AI powered tool will be needed. But in order to get this into the production environment, this AI driven tool will first need to learn and be thoroughly trained on what previous false positives have looked like. Then, it will of course need to be tested, to make sure that it delivers the desired output. This will have to be done in a test environment, which is isolated from the rest of the IT and network infrastructure. At the present time, there are a number of cybervendors that offer this kind of AI driven filtering tool. But to build our proposed solution, we will examine the solution that is offered by Scylla AI. To view more information about this, see: http://cyberresources.solutions/GenAI_Book/AI_Filter ing.pdf

- The SIEM:
Assuming that the AI filtering tool for false positives has been deemed to be a success, and has been deployed in the production environment, it will then connect to what is known as a "SIEM". This is an acronym that stands for "Security Information and Event Management". It can be technically defined as follows:

The underlying principles of every SIEM system are to aggregate relevant data from multiple sources, identify deviations from the norm and take appropriate action.[3]

Thus, the primary purpose of the SIEM is to collect all of the legitimate (or authentic) warnings and alerts that have been ascertained by the AI filtering tool and present them to the IT security team in a holistic fashion, through just one console for quick viewing. Thus, as mentioned earlier, this will lead to an effective and efficient methodology of triaging, which should help in cutting down the Mean Time To Detect time frame, which is right now at seven months.

For the purposes of our proposed solution, we are anticipating using the SIEM package that is available from Exabeam. To view more information about this platform, see: http://cyb erresources.solutions/GenAI_Book/SIEM.pdf

- The Digital Person:
This was reviewed in extensive detail in Chapter 3. But in terms of our proposed solution, the SIEM will now connect to the Digital Person, and once the authentic or legitimate warnings and alerts have been processed and triaged, the most critical will then be transmitted to the Digital Person. In return, this persona will verbally alert the IT security team so that they will take immediate notice of it. This Digital Person will also be powered by Generative AI and Natural Language Processing, concepts reviewed in Chapter 2. In this role, the Digital Person serves two distinct purposes:

* By verbally communicating the authentic or legitimate warnings and alerts, they will be brought to the attention of the IT security team immediately, rather than relying on them noticing them on the SIEM for whatever reason.
* Also, the communications with the Digital Person will be two-way. This means that a member of the IT security team will also be able to talk to the Digital Person and instruct it on what to do. This will be examined more closely in the next two components.

For this component of the proposed solution, we are anticipating using the platform that is available from Soul Machines. By using their Soul Machines Studio, a Digital Person can be created and configured to meet the needs of our proposed solution. More information about this can be seen at:
www.soulmachines.com/soul-machines-studio
- The Holistic Cyber Solution:
This will be an all encompassing package with the primary objective of having triggers to stop a phishing attack (or for that matter any other kind or type of threat variant). This in turn will be connected to the Digital Person. For example, if the Digital Person is triggered by the SIEM package that a phishing attack is underway and has alerted the IT security team to this effect, then all that a team member will have to do is merely instruct the Digital Person to deprovision all of the accounts that reside in the Privileged Access account server

(which will be reviewed next). From there, the Digital Person will then activate the Holistic Cyber Solution to launch the triggers and mechanisms to actually make this happen.

For this component, we are anticipating using the platform that is available from Darktrace. To view information about this, see:

http://cyberresources.solutions/GenAI_Book/Holistic_Cyber_Solutions.pdf

- The Privileged Access Management Server:

This is also referred to as the "PAM" server. This is where all of the Privileged Access accounts will reside and can be set up, deprovisioned, modified, scaled up, scaled down, etc. The Holistic Cyber Solution will in turn be connected to the PAM server. So, if a member of the IT security team gets the alert or warning from the Digital Person that a phishing attack is indeed underway, in turn, that same person will instruct the Digital Person to deprovision all of the Privileged Access accounts. This will activate the triggers in the Holistic Cyber Solution, and from there, it will communicate with the PAM server to deactivate all of the accounts. It is important to note that all of the Privileged Access accounts will remain in a deactivated state until the phishing attack has actually been contained. Once this happens, the member of the IT security team will tell the Digital Person to do the reverse, which then launch the triggers to activate all of the Privileged Access accounts again.

For this part of the solution, we are anticipating utilizing the services from CyberArk. They have a platform in the Azure Marketplace that can be deployed and configured as a PAM based server. To view more information about this, see:

http://cyberresources.solutions/GenAI_Book/PAM_Server.pdf

The entire process can be seen in Figure 5.1:

Other Potential Use Cases

Finally, as mentioned, this proposed solution is still in the theoretical phase. It will have to be tested in a controlled environment with live

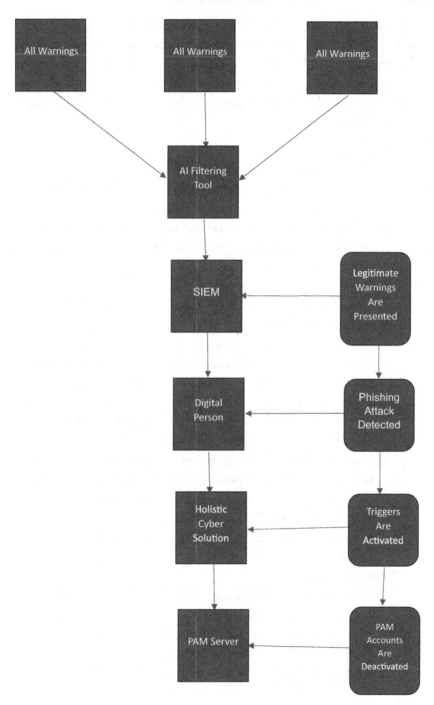

Figure 5.1 How the Digital Person can be used to reduce the MTTD and the MTTR.

data. In order to accomplish this task, we are anticipating making use of Microsoft Azure to deploy these components in a Virtual Data Center. But over time, if this proposed solution does prove to be viable, it has other potential applications as well, especially in the area of Identity and Access Management (also known as "IAM"). These include the following:

1) Authentication:
   - Adaptive and Continuous User Authentication.
   - Advancing the use of biometrics as an authentication mechanism in Multifactor Authentication solutions.
   - Continuous and Adaptive Authentication. This simply means that the employee login session can be continuously monitored, taking into account other contextual data.

2) Authorization:
   - Creating "intelligent" Role-Based Access Controls (also known as "RBACs").
   - Greater enforcement of the concept of "least privilege".
   - Role Mining and Optimization: This will lead to a decrease in over-assigning rights, privileges, and permissions.
   - Dynamic Access Controls: This is where the rights, permissions, and privileges can be assigned on a real time basis, thus supporting the concept of "Just In Time".
   - Customization of Role-Based Access Controls: This is where the rights, permissions, and privileges can be customized and tailored to what was used in the past.
   - Forward Thinking: This methodology could serve as a model as to what the future rights, permissions, and privileges can look like.

3) Administration:
   - Automated User Management: This is where the employee can manage their own rights, permissions, and privileges, with approval and oversight from the IT security team.
   - Role-Based Access Control Automation: This is where the entire RBAC process can be driven by AI and thus be fully automated.

- Intelligent End User Profile Management: This is where Generative AI can be used to predict what future user profiles will look like. This will be especially useful for the Active Directory in Azure.

Notes

1 www.rapid7.com/fundamentals/kerberoasting-attack/
2 https://saviynt.com/glossary/just-in-time-access
3 www.techtarget.com/searchsecurity/definition/security-information-and-event-management-SIEM

Index

Note: Page numbers in **bold** refer to tables and those in *italic* refer to figures.

Printed in the United States
by Baker & Taylor Publisher Services